IRON HOUSE

Stories from the Yard

Jerome Washington

QED Press
Fort Bragg, California

Iron House: Stories from the Yard
© 1994 by Jerome Washington

Portions of this book have appeared in *Contact II*, *The Transatlantic Review*, *Witness* and *A Bright Spot in the Yard* (Crossing Press, 1981).

For their support and expertise, QED Press thanks publicist Belvie Rooks, editor John Fremont, designer Mark Gatter, photographer Malcolm Davis, advisor Sal Glynn, and bookseller Tony Miksak.

Iron House: Stories from the Yard received the Western States Book Award for Creative Nonfiction in 1994. The Western States Book Awards are a project of the Western States Arts Federation. The awards are supported by The Xerox Foundation and Crane Duplicating Services. Additional funding is provided by the National Endowment for the Arts.

Library of Congress Cataloging-in-Publication Data
Washington, Jerome, 1939–
 Iron house : stories from the yard / Jerome Washington.
  p. cm.
 ISBN 0-936609-33-8
 1. Prisoners—New York (State)—Literary collections.
 2. Prisons—New York (State)—Literary collections. 3. New York (State)—Social conditions. 4. Attica Correctional Facility
 I. Title.
 PS3573.A7935I76   1994
 365'.44'0974793—dc20   94-10662
                                                          CIP

Cover photograph by Malcolm Davis
Cover design by Mark Gatter

To order single copies of *Iron House*, please send $18.95 (California residents add $1.37 sales tax) plus $2 (4th class) or $3 (UPS) for shipping and handling to:

QED Press
155 Cypress Street
Fort Bragg, CA 95437

For information, phone (707) 964-9520. For bookseller and library discounts or VISA and MasterCard orders, please call 800/773-7782.

Printed in the United States of America
First Edition, October 1994
10 9 8 7 6 5 4 3 2

To J. Emily Zukerberg for her keen insight and literary prowess, and to the memory of Etheridge Knight—poet, shaman, pathfinder.

Acknowledgments

For their support and encouragement, the author extends special thanks to Kathrin Perutz, Tino Perutz, Gwendolyn Brooks, Fielding Dawson, Paul Krassner, Piri Thomas, Edward Hower, Norman Mailer, Geri Lipschultz, Joyce Jenkins, Cathy Lee Crane, Albertha Furby Walker, Elizabeth E. Lewis, Hytha Rice and the Writers Fund Committee, PEN American Center.

For their creative influence, the author pays homage to Jackie McLean, John Coltrane, Elvin Ray Jones, Max Roach, Ishmael Reed, Amiri Baraka, Hattie Gossett and the late Bob Thompson.

Preface

IN PRISON, life is hard-edged and authority is capricious, thoughts are contraband and writing is a deadly, serious business.

The imprisoned writer does not have the luxury of writing to entertain, nor to write as a matter of commercial adventurism. Every word must count. There can be no waste, no fat, and there is no second chance.

Prison writers are often called liars and troublemakers by the officials. The most effective writers are slandered as terrorists who plan to overthrow the warden's administration. Their writings are banned from distribution within the prison and referred to as "venom." This is perhaps the best review a prison writer can ever expect from a prison official.

Prison writers are sometimes "put on the boat": shipped without notice from prison to prison. Their bodies are abused; their lives are disrupted; their human rights are disregarded and their writings are confiscated and destroyed.

Still they write. Not because writing is therapeutic or that it will open the gates to freedom. Prison writers write for the same reason that writers everywhere write—because it is life saving!

In one prison, the warden ordered a full-scale shakedown in which every cell was thoroughly searched. Everything, including the beds, was dismantled. The prison guards were not searching for weapons or illegal drugs. On the contrary, the dangerous contraband they sought were the manuscripts of prisoners who wrote about inhumane prison conditions.

No other class of writers in America is subjected to the totalitarian controls placed on the writers in our prisons. Prison controls are absolute, even to the point of when and where inmates may use a toilet. As a result of this repression, writers in prison have learned to survive the situation, not rationalize it. They write *from* the prison experience, not about the experience. It is this particular point of view which sets the prison writer apart from all others.

Prison life forces an involvement with the subject, and prison writers cannot deal in myths or stereotypes. Readers outside may be fooled, but if the writing is not representative and doesn't ring true to fellow prisoners, criticism can come from the blade of a knife or a punch in the face.

The line is clear and clean between that which is born from experience and that which is reported from the safety of an observation deck.

Jerome Washington

American Justice

Those of us who are in prison
have been convicted.
Everyone else is still on trial.

Moe Jones

"AIN'T NOTHING CRYPTIC or subtle about this place," Moe Jones, the inmate clothing clerk, said as he issued my first prison uniform. "Everything is up front. Direct. To the point and for real."

I pulled on the pants he had given me. They were too short, and the shirt was too tight.

"Fits you like a dream," Moe said between puffs of cigar smoke. Then he issued me a king size sheet for my pint size bed. "You'll shrink to fit the clothes," Moe said. "As for the extra large sheet, that's in case you decide to hang yourself. There'll be plenty left to cover the body."

◆

For you who can't imagine what it's like to be in a cell, lock yourself in a closet. Think of all the things you enjoyed most in life. Now reach out and ask yourself: "Where are they?"

◆

When the Man takes your name and gives you a number, the first thing you have to adjust to is not who you are but how many digits you have become.

◆

Most prisoners know the rules which govern them much better than most guards whose job it is to enforce those rules. There is nothing confusing about this. In prison it's a normal situation. Just a simple matter of the oppressed knowing more about the nature of his oppression than the oppressor.

There is little wonder that when a guard is at a loss for the exact rule he feels has been violated, he often substitutes a handy lie for the truth.

Ignorance dictates. In most cases, prison discipline is more a matter of making up rules to create a crime than matching a crime to the written rule.

◆

Turning the corner into the prison yard for the first time is like stepping onto the set of a Cecil B. DeMille spectacular where most of the extras are black.

Everyone has a yard image. Still there are no plush trimmings, trumpet fanfares or superstars. The only Herculean act performed is survival.

I scan the yard for a friendly face. There is none, yet one is familiar. He doesn't recognize me so I don't speak. But the next time I see him strolling the avenue, flashing fake diamonds and draped in dyed rabbit, he'll not convince me that he was vacationing in Miami or Vegas. I know where he has disappeared to. I am here also.

The thirty-foot-high walls tell me that yesterday was a better day.

◆

The secrets of American justice are learned in dark places, like prison cells.

Clutch Cargo

Victoria Delrina was one of the first female guards assigned duty in an all-male prison. She was a natural blonde, a
Virgo, and though she wasn't unattractive, she was trapped
somewhere between absolutely homely and almost good-
looking. However, she had an ass wide enough to earn her the
moniker of Clutch Cargo.

When the sun was hot, prisoners standing idle in the
shade along the cellblock walls tracked the slow, smooth
swing of her flared hips as she patrolled the crowded exercise
yard. We had to constantly remind ourselves and each other
that while Clutch Cargo was a full-figured woman with the
scent of fresh rose buds, she was nevertheless a prison guard.
There was also big danger in staring for too long. A prisoner
could be punished as severely for "reckless eyeballing" as he
would be for attempting to escape.

Most male guards resented Clutch Cargo's invasion of
their previously all-male turf. Her presence was a threat to
their image. Her pleasant voice and smile were a contrast to
the aggressive swagger of bigger, stronger male guards. She
didn't carry a nightstick, and because she walked the same
ground as they did, male guards could no longer moan about
the dangers of their job. "She won't last much longer," a guard
sergeant said. It was a hope that became a prayer.

After the courts ruled that women have the same rights
of employment as men and cannot be barred because of their
sex, rumors were spread to discredit her and force her to re-
sign. Mud-slinging guards told prisoners that Clutch Cargo
was a heavy drinker, an undercover alcoholic. Some claimed,
though none admitted firsthand knowledge, that she had
been a voluntary sex slave at a three-day orgy. Other gossip
labeled her a lesbian, a diesel dyke who liked little girls, and

once a pig-faced hack named Geldman intentionally misdi-
rected her into a room where a line of prisoners stood naked while their clothing was being searched for
contraband. Of course, Geldman apologized to her face for
his "mistake," but he and his buddies cracked laughing behind her back.

When Clutch Cargo first entered the crowded mess hall
at noon and headed toward her post at the front, Geldman
urged a few flunky prisoners to start a series of cat-calls. Like
waves gathering intensity, other prisoners added their whistles, and everyone cheered Clutch Cargo's walk between the
rows of tables as if rooting for a stripper strutting a burlesque
runway. After a minute or two, before the cheers turned
nasty, Geldman and his buddies stepped in to quiet the prisoners and restore order. They were heroes to the rescue, but
their damage had already been done. Clutch Cargo's face was
livid red, her body trembled with anger and she bit blood
from her lower lip to keep from crying.

Every day for a week, Clutch Cargo received the same
treatment. Then, one day, when cat-calls and whistles had
reached a peak, she shocked everyone by striking back.

Clutch Cargo shrugged away her embarrassment, strode
determinedly to the front of the mess hall, and without a hint
of hesitation, she climbed onto the stainless steel serving
counter and took a bow.

Everyone was struck dumb; every mouth was hushed.

"My kind of woman," Shithouse Shorty said to Chink
Wade. "Lotta heart!"

"Yeah," Chink replied, "She's got balls."

♦

New breed guards seldom beat with clubs. Modern penology is not that personal. The system does a number on the brain cavity that creates psychological cripples.

A wounded mind takes longer to heal; the scars last forever.

♦

Every prison has a "Shorty," a "Heavy," a few "Slims," a couple of "Chicos," one or more guys calling themselves "Brother," and an assortment of "Juniors" and "Youngbloods."

The same names recur from prison to prison like set moves in a game of chess. Each has a story behind it. Each has a reason and logic for being.

"Hard Luck Henry" was busted on Friday the 13th by an off-duty cop. "Bitedown" bit his lover's cock off. "Boxhead Mike's" name speaks for itself. "Wizard" can make wine out of Kool Aid. If push comes to shove, he can get high on mess hall soup and a long conversation. "Waco" is as wild as a cowboy playing hopscotch. He hasn't cooled down yet. "Loco Larry" is a space-case and "Pop" is the oldest man in the cell block. Every name fits, including "Conjugal John." By hook, crook, beg or pay, John has had every queen in the prison.

♦

The new-jack, rookie guard knows he's supposed to be doing something to earn his pay, but he's not sure exactly what.

He looks official in his shiny black shoes and his new blue uniform with his polished oak nightstick swinging from the loop on his belt. He patrols up one side of the exercise yard and down the other. His swagger is an imitation from a

James Cagney movie and his on-the-job training is a parody
of older guards. He hopes he's doing the right thing. If not,
he'll continue doing wrong because no one knows how to
teach him what's right.

The rookie walks his route, watching without understanding what he's supposed to be watching for. At the first
sign of trouble he'll either cower like a turtle, pulling in his
head for protection, or he'll overreact and kill as many prisoners as possible.

Prison leaves the rookie guard as few options for survival as it does a prisoner—perhaps even fewer.

◆

Summer comes strange to prison.

Spring passes along the handball courts, makes a U-turn
below guardtower number twelve, then follows winter to the
death house exit.

Summer yawns up: a cat stretching the sleep away. Not
wanting pets, just to be left alone, it settles into a warm ball
and waits the next move.

Autumn lurks in the wings.

◆

Prison is an oral place. There's not much to look at in a
cell, so inmates do a lot of talking. They talk to their neighbor,
or the guy locked five cells away, two above, or one below.

Even in the yard, it's an oral place. Jiving. Joking. Shout-
ing. Laughing. Crying. Often just plain lying.

Inmates will rap about anything, to anyone, to keep the
tension off of them. And when no one else will give us any
rap, we talk to ourselves.

Fast-Walkin' Willie

Fast-Walkin' Willie's jitterbug self is empty of meaning. When he opens his mouth to speak, contradictions leap out. He can double-talk, slick-talk, and con cheese from a rat, but Willie can't read a word, or even write his own name.

Willie copped out. He pled guilty to "all known and unknown crimes." The prosecutor shrewdly used Willie's ignorance to clear the books of unsolved crimes, and now Willie's doing time for muggers who didn't get caught.

In prison, Fast-Walkin' Willie happily takes the slaver's bit and even taps his top to the cadence of their call.

Fast-Walkin' Willie is exactly what the guards love to see.

◆

We are stacked in tiers in darkened cells. Our hushed conversations romanticize the past. We hook into the memories of females like butchers hooking meat.

Our fantasies power us and drag us through the emasculated night. We remember broads and chicks, good-time girls in red skirts with tails sashaying through afterhour club nights. We recall the fast-life smiles on painted lips and smooth, rounded flanks dancing in spiked shoes. We remember the dreams and the myths, but few of us can ever remember dealing with a real woman.

◆

Small Things.

"Hello."

"Good morning."

They're the last things you miss. But when they're gone you've begun to understand what Attica is about.

Maxwell, Chink Wade and Pete Moss

Chink Wade and Pete Moss were pushing pieces around a chess board on a table in the main yard when Maxwell interrupted.

"We're going to meet with the warden," Maxwell said, shifting his clipboard of papers from one hand to the other.

" 'We,' who?" Chink Wade asked.

"The Liaison Committee," Maxwell answered, then added, "you guys have any suggestions or complaints we should lay on him?"

Maxwell was president of the Inmate Liaison Committee, elected to represent prisoners in meetings with the warden and other officials. The warden euphemistically referred to the Committee as the "democratic voice of the inmate population," but among prisoners the Committee's effectiveness was always in doubt. No matter how valid a complaint, after a perfunctory review, the warden usually sneered and summarily dismissed it as a petty gripe.

"Won't do no good," Chink Wade frowned as he advanced a pawn on the chessboard. "Warden never hears what we gotta say. He's gonna do whatever he wants, regardless."

"Yeah, that's right," Pete Moss concurred. He moved a knight capturing Chink's pawn, putting the queen's bishop under attack and threatening checkmate. "Seems the more we beef, the tighter his rules get. He done already made more new rules in the last two months than his guards can enforce, or we can live by."

"And you gotta know," Chink said as he carefully studied the chessboard and considered his next move, "this warden ain't cool at all." As he countered Pete's move, saving his bishop from capture and protecting his king from checkmate, Chink added, "If 'n you need proof, just look what he done yesterday. He even made a new rule to govern the old rules."

"That's exactly why we're meeting with him today," Maxwell said.

"Won't do no good," Chink repeated his admonition. "He takes pleasure in posting rules to make us squirm. He loves screwing us."

"That's a truth." Pete Moss captured another of Chink's pawns. "If the warden don't do it to his wife at night, he'll sure as hell do it to us in the morning."

Both Chink and Pete laughed, but Chink stopped laughing when Pete Moss captured still another piece and forced Chink's queen to retreat to safety.

"Anyway," Pete Moss said as he sized up his next move, "the warden only holds these meetings so he can see if his rules are working. He wants to look on your faces, that's all."

"Why does he want to see our faces?" Maxwell asked, looking from Chink to Pete Moss then back to Chink for an answer.

" 'Cause he gets a nut just seeing the pain and suffering on your faces." Chink moved his king's bishop, putting Pete Moss' left flank under attack. "You're the warden's barometer."

"How's that?" Maxwell naïvely asked.

Pete Moss grinned. "He can judge from your committee how well he's zooming the rest of us."

"And you gotta know," said Chink Wade, "he comes all over himself 'cause he's got us by the balls."

"And he's squeezing hard," Pete Moss chuckled triumphantly as he ended the game by putting Chink's king in checkmate.

♦

"When I go home at night," the cell block guard said, "I forget about this place. I leave my job on the job." He wiped the sweat from his thick red neck and relit his cigar stub. "If I were to think of you prisoners as human beings, no different from my wife and kids, I'd never be able to lock you in a cell. Then where would I be?" He flicked his cigar ash on the clean floor then answered his own question. "I would be on welfare because opening and closing cells and counting heads are the only things I know."

I remembered hearing that a guard's job was the highest paid unskilled job in the state, so I couldn't feel sorry for him.

He flicked another chunk of ash, then ordered me to sweep it up before the duty sergeant reported him for having a dirty cell block floor.

Dennis

Dennis went directly from the womb to prison.

He was the child of a child. His mother was a fourteen-year-old girl who thought it cute to be pregnant until morning sickness racked her young body, and Dennis arrived before her monthly welfare check could be cashed.

There was no baseball, or hide 'n' seek, or playing tag in Dennis' young life. Neither was there any joy in growing older.

Dennis was taught street-life while still in diapers, and he learned to hustle drugs before he could recite the alphabet.

The sidewalk was his playground. It was a sliding board that went quickly downhill.

Right from wrong was a luxury reserved for boys with full stomachs and warm socks. For Dennis, the end always justified the means. Situations were meant to survive, not rationalize. It was wrong to go hungry.

His mother didn't fail him. She was too young to know how to fail. His failure started before his birth, and it was reinforced in life.

Now Dennis recites his ABC's while pressing automobile license plates, and he learns right from wrong from the prison rulebook.

♦

Everything is a shade of grey. That's the color of prison.

The sky is grey. The walls are sand-grey. The yard is grey-black asphalt, and the inmates' uniforms, which appear green, are also shades of grey.

Grey controls all. It gets into the mood, the spirit, and even the food has a grey bland taste.

It is no accident that grey is the chosen color; the color scheme is an integral part of any controller's plan. Grey neutralizes, represses and debilitates.

In prison, grey dominates.

♦

How is a prisoner supposed to be objective about his plight? It's as much of a folly to ask that of a prisoner as to ask it of a man who has his nuts caught in a slam-locked door. Neither can be objective about the pain. And neither should be asked to be objective.

♦

"You ain't got to tell me about pain," Old Man Fish grunted. "I've been here for twenty-three years and you don't know what hurting is until you try acting as if it doesn't hurt."

♦

Junior

They stood around, goading Junior on like ranch hands
cheering a bronc buster.

"Don't take no shit from the Man," one said.

Another added, "Your manhood is at stake."

Junior, whose flanks had never known the warmth of a
woman's thighs, whose youth was still in his voice, swung at
a uniformed guard and was dragged off, feet first, to be gang
stomped in the privacy of the guardhouse.

After Junior was gone and the blood had been washed
away, they stood around like overfed vultures, burping that
Junior was a sucker for listening to them. All the same, they
kept an eye out for another hunk of young pigmeat to throw
against the guards.

♦

"Sure," the old line guard spat a gob of tobacco juice into
a tin cup as he explained to the new recruit fresh on the job
from the training academy, "I know which prisoners are making booze. I know which are fucking the fags. I know which
are smoking dope and breaking all the other rules, too. I
know everything everybody is doing. That's my job." He gave
a smug smile, then spat another gob of tobacco juice into the
cup. "But so what?" he smirked. "Ain't nobody killing nobody
and ain't nobody trying to escape."

The old line guard read the confusion on the recruit's
face, patted him on the back and proclaimed, "As long as
they're happy not trying to get out, I'm happy letting them
break the rules."

The young guard was staggered. His mouth hung open
like the rear flap on a dump truck. He was hearing everything
the academy had trained him against.

"Just remember," the old timer said as he offered the recruit a plug of tobacco, "you can't stop everything and run a good prison too."

After a few more on-the-job training sessions the new recruit learned to get along by going along, to pass the buck and cover his ass. He also learned to chew tobacco, shoot the juice with amazing accuracy, look the other way and get a slice of the pie in the process.

Diamond Bob

Two days after Diamond Bob came to Sing-Sing he was called in to meet with the Program Committee—three civilian officials who assign prisoners to work stations or educational programs.

The Committee's chairperson picked Diamond Bob's file from the pile of folders on the long wooden table and thumbed through it. After moments of indecision, he frowned at what he saw and put the folder aside.

"Do you have a trade?" the chairperson asked Diamond Bob.

Diamond Bob slouched in his seat. He paid more attention to his fingernails than he did to the chairperson, projecting an attitude that let everybody know he'd been through this procedure many times before, and that he was bored.

"Do you have any skills?" the chairperson went on. "Plumbing, bricklaying, cutting hair? Anything at all?"

"Sure," Diamond Bob said, "I'm skilled. I'm highly trained." And then without the slightest hesitation, he added, "I've got a Ph.D. in G."

The chairperson's face screwed up as he looked to the other committee members for understanding, but they were no help. One was engrossed in furious note-taking, while the other sat like a dunce with confusion stamped on his face.

"You have a Ph.D. in *what?*" The chairperson leaned forward with elbows on the table, trying to unravel the riddle.

" *'G'.*" Diamond Bob was indignant. "Don't you know what 'G' is?"

The three Committee members all confessed their ignorance.

" 'G' stands for 'Game'," Diamond Bob proclaimed with a casual flip of his fingertips, "And Game is what we pimps, players and fast-life hustlers do for a living. Game is older than the pyramids and faster than lightning. We play it in the streets, in bars, with fast women and fancy cars. Our Game is called 'G' for short."

"I see," the chairperson said, exchanging snide smiles with the two other committee members. "And you have a Ph.D. in this Game of yours. Is that correct?"

"Sure do. I'm a grandmaster." Diamond Bob, tuned in to his own hype, puffed with pride. "Women sell their product, and I manage their affairs."

"What product?" the committee member who looked like a dunce asked.

"Flesh!" Diamond Bob said, "Body flesh. What other product does a woman have?"

Everybody except Diamond Bob fidgeted in his chair.

"Your Game is not what I had in mind," the chairperson said, "I'm asking about work skills."

Bob was annoyed, but maintained his cool. "Game is work. Ain't no work more skilled," he said, "and on top of my skill, I gotta be cold-blooded to do what I do for a living."

"I don't doubt that," the chairperson interrupted.

Bob shoved the comment aside and went on rappin'.

"I'm the guy who'll hang a rope, kill a rock and drown a glass of water." He snapped his fingers to an unheard beat. "It's ''hoe money, or no money.' That's my code."

"What you're talking about is a curse," the chairperson snapped, "That's not an honest living; that's pandering."

Diamond Bob was undaunted. He held his ground. "You asked my profession, and I told the truth." He offered a proposition. "Now, if you got any women in this prison who want to peddle their ass, then call on me—because I'm a qualified pimp. Otherwise," he sneered, "don't offer me none of your plantation gigs. I don't get my fingernails dirty for no-body. Can you dig *that?*"

The chairperson was livid. He balled his fist until the knuckles turned white and stamped a foot on the floor. The two other committee members tried to calm him, reminding him about his high blood pressure. The chairperson shook them off and shouted in Diamond Bob's face. "Get out!" he boomed and jabbed a finger toward the door.

The next morning, even before the sun could knock the night's chill off the exercise yard, Diamond Bob was on his way to see the prison shrink.

"I ain't insane," Diamond Bob repeated as a phalanx of guards escorted him through the prison corridors, "I got a Ph.D. in 'G'. I'm a businessman, an entrepreneur. I'm living the American Dream."

◆

The real horror of prison is not the torment of human flesh, but the system that tolerates it.

◆

Cleanhead Meets Dale Carnegie

I was coming down the long stairway from the tailor's shop above the prison's bathhouse when I met September Red and Fast Eddie the Gypper coming up. They were carrying bundles of inmate uniforms to be repaired and reissued. This was their once-a-day assignment, and they went about it with the same haphazard air as any other inmate would—just a way of passing the time.

"Hey, now, Jay," Red said. He held out his right hand, palm up.

"What it is?" I slapped his hand in greeting.

"Same old, same old."

"Nothing changed but the address," Fast Eddie said. "Everything's for real."

I knew the feeling and said so.

"Johnson's back," Red said as he lowered his bundle to the stairs.

"Which Johnson?"

"Cleanhead," Fast Eddie answered. He hiked his bundle higher, more comfortably on his back.

"No shit," I said. "When did he show?"

"This morning. Two marshals brought him back," Red said, then asked for a cigarette.

I shook one free from my pack. He dropped it into his pocket and said he'd smoke it later.

"Was it a parole violation?"

"Naw," Fast Eddie said, "the dude's got a brand new beef."

"Shit."

"Two-and-a-half to five."

"And he still owed a deuce on his old sentence," Red added.

"What's the bust for this trip?"

"Same old stuff," Fast Eddie said. "Snatching other folk's stuff in the middle of the night."

"Burglary?"

"That's what the law calls it."

"Had to be," Fast Eddie said. "Cleanhead didn't live there and he sure as hell didn't have no key."

"Damn shame," I said. "Cleanhead just left here three months ago."

"He's back now," Red said.

A guard coming up the stairs squeezed past us. He went a few steps higher, then turned and in a shaky but gruff tone told us to move on.

"Don't panic," Red mumbled. "We ain't plotting."

"What was that?" The guard stepped up another step, putting a little more space between us, but his voice was harsher. "You some kind of smart ass?"

"No," Red stared up at him. "We're just taking these things to the tailor's shop."

"Then get on with it," the guard snarled as he backed up a few more steps, then turned and climbed on toward the top.

Red chuckled and lifted his bundle onto his shoulder.

"Some dudes feel better in prison than out," Fast Eddie said as he and Red started up the stairs again.

"Don't think that's Cleanhead's problem." I flattened against the wall so they could pass.

"What is?" Red asked.

"He just don't know how not to get busted."

Fast Eddie laughed. "That's his problem, yours, mine, Red's and everybody else's in the joint."

"That's the real deal," I said. Looking up at them, I asked, "Where is he?"

"C Block. Reception Company," Red shouted back as they went up.

I pushed open C Block's door and looked around for the guard. He wasn't in sight.

"Cleanhead's back," Big Shorty, the Reception Company clerk, said as I stepped inside.

"I got the wire," I said. "What cell is he in?"

"Eight-twenty-five. But you can't see him."

"No?"

"He'll be locked in 'til the Security Office okays him for the yard."

"When will that be?"

"Tomorrow sometime."

"Can I run down and yell at him?"

"Not with McGraw on duty," Big Shorty lowered his voice. "That redneck would put us both in segregation."

We agreed that McGraw was a motherfucker.

"Tight. By the book," Big Shorty said. "He sees evil in everything."

We heard keys jingling, knew that McGraw had finished his rounds and was headed back to the reception desk.

"When you get a chance," I said quickly, "give Cleanhead my hello."

"Sure thing."

"If he needs anything, let me know."

Big Shorty nodded.

I stepped through the door, out into the bright sun, and went across the main yard to the gym for my afternoon workout.

It was two days later and raining when I ran into Cleanhead. He had just come from the barber shop where he had

had his head freshly shaved, his scalp shampooed, massaged and oiled.

"Damn sorry to see you back."

"That's two of us," Cleanhead said.

The rain formed into beads on his slippery head, then slid down onto his jacket collar.

"What went down?" I asked.

"Got caught behind enemy lines without proper ID," he joked.

We walked through the control gate, showed our passes to the guard, then started across the yard toward the library.

"Seriously."

"Can't figure it out," Cleanhead said.

We flashed "peace" and "power" signs at two other inmates going in the opposite direction. They returned the greetings.

"Did a good job," he said. "Didn't break a glass. Didn't make a sound. Didn't leave a fingerprint."

"A clean job is your trademark," I said.

Big Shorty hurried toward us. He was all hassled and blown out of shape, splashing through the puddles and struggling to keep his balance, a goat jumping rope backwards.

"What you doing out in the rain?" I shouted at Big Shorty.

"That fucking McGraw is sending me for supplies."

"Somebody's got to do it," I said as he neared.

"Ain't my job," Big Shorty wiped the rain from his forehead. "McGraw is being a prick."

"He's a hack," Cleanhead said. "That's his role."

"Just hold your peace," I said to Big Shorty as he came abreast and passed us. "Everything will be cool."

"Shit," Big Shorty snorted. He waved his pass at the guard and splashed on through the control gate.

At the library we shook the rain from our jackets and went in. A few guys were reading newspapers and magazines, others were wearing headphones, snapping their fingers to the music and mouthing the lyrics as they listened, but most were just keeping out of the rain. We took two books from the shelf and sat at a side table with the books open in front of us.

I asked Cleanhead again how the bust went down.

"That," he emphasized the word, "I still can't figure. Everything was smooth, like polished glass."

"Maybe a sick junkie ratted you out for a fix?"

We kept our voices low, giving the guard no reason to hassle us.

"Naw," he said. "Nobody knew about the job but me."

"And, of course, the police and the victim."

"That was after the fact," he said. "I just can't figure how they knew it was me." He fluttered the pages of the book with his thumb, then let it lay open at a random page. "It was a clean job." There was the edge of pride in his voice. "It was polished. Brilliant. I was Rembrandt creating a masterpiece." He fluttered the pages again, then shut the book and pushed it from him. "I left no traces," he said. "I only took things I knew I could get rid of quickly. I checked and rechecked everything. Still, three days later, the police showed at my place and busted me."

"Think carefully," I said. "Something's got to fit. The police ain't psychic. They don't use a Ouija board."

He shook his head and shrugged and said, "Hell, Jay, I did it the same as I always do a job."

We leaned back in our chairs and were quiet for a long while. Then I said, "That's your answer."

"What's my answer?"

"Your super-clean, smooth, professional M.O."

"My what?"

"Your modus operandi. That's Latin," I said.

"I know it's Latin. Now run it to me in English."

"Your mode of operation." I broke it down for him. "Your method of doing a job.

His defenses shot up. "I always do a professional job." There was an irate edge to his voice. "I'm never sloppy and I do all burglaries the same way."

"And that's what got you busted."

"Being professional?"

"No," I said. "Not being professional enough got you busted."

"Bullshit," Cleanhead said. "I'm a pro. A real pro."

"Ain't no pros in prison."

"Fuck you, Jay," he said and stood up.

"Sit down. Relax and listen."

He sat down slowly but stayed tense and on the edge of his chair.

"A real pro," I said, "never does the same thing twice. He always changes his routine. Invents new ways." If I had learned nothing else in prison, I learned that, I told him. "You didn't learn, and now you're back in the joint."

He stared at me. Cold. Then his defensive shield left him; he slid back in his chair and was ready to talk again.

"What else could it be?" I leaned closer to him. "No witnesses. No rats. Nothing. And the stuff you took couldn't be traced. Right?"

He nodded and said slowly, "So the only thing they had to go on was the way I did the job."

"Right."

"And that's what got me busted, huh?"

"All they had to do was check the files and fit the method and the burglar together."

"And I fit."

"Must be, 'cause must ain't don't sound right," I said, "and you being back here is proof enough."

"Damn," he said and leaned far back in his chair.

Three weeks later, Cleanhead was assigned to the school's office as a clerk. He couldn't type, couldn't file and knew nothing about keeping records. But he was jailwise and knew how to tell the Job Assignment Committee what they wanted to hear.

"Hey, Jay," Cleanhead called me to a halt as I was coming from the mess hall.

I stepped toward him. "How's the job?" I asked.

"It's an all day gig, but it beats slaving in the license plate shop."

"True."

We stepped aside to make way for guys returning a load of empty food trays from SHU—the Segregation Housing Unit—to the mess hall.

"Best thing is," Cleanhead said, "I get a lot of free time to do my own thing."

"That's hip. A dude's personal program is far more important than the official one the Man sets up."

The loudspeakers sounded: "Return to shops, school and cell blocks. The yard is closed." A guard moving casually, but with a mission, told a small group to move on. Another guard came in our direction.

"Which way you headed?" I asked Cleanhead.

"School," he said. "Back to work."

"I'll give you a walk over."

Just as the guard opened his mouth to speak, we moved off.

"I'm re-digging my role," Cleanhead said as we walked toward the school yard gate. "Checking out new angles and pulling loose ends together."

"Prison is time for re-grouping."

"That M.O. thing could have me coming back to prison for the rest of my natural life." We waved to September Red and Fast Eddie the Gypper. They were struggling with their bundles, going toward the tailor's shop. "And the worst part," Cleanhead said, "I wouldn't even know why."

"Most guys ain't hip to it. Some never will be."

"Glad you turned me on," he said. "I thought I was a pro, but I was nothing but popcorn."

We went through the gate, were counted in by the guard, crossed the school yard, went inside, went down the hall and into the school office.

"I got a lot of rebuilding to do," Cleanhead said as he eased into the chair behind his desk.

"We've all got that to do." I sat on the edge of the desk. "There ain't no success stories in prison."

"This is one that's going to be a success." He pulled open a desk drawer and handed me a full-page Dale Carnegie ad torn from a magazine. The line *"Learn to utilize your abilities more effectively"* was underlined and circled in red. "You hip to this dude?" he asked.

"Yeah, I know about D.C.," I joked. "It's a course for white collar con players." Then I asked, "You planning to get into it?"

"Already ordered the book." He dropped the ad back into the drawer and slid it shut. "When I hit the streets this time, my shit is really going to be on high point."

Three guys came into the office and asked about changes in class schedules. Cleanhead referred them to the clerk across the room.

"No more picking locks and climbing in other folks' windows." He leaned back with his hands cupped behind his head. "I'm changing my game completely," he said. "I'll be dipping into a new trick bag for each job I do. With this D.C. jive under my belt, I'll be coming off so slick at the mouth the victims will thank me for choosing them."

An educational counselor leaned in through the door and asked Cleanhead to locate a student.

"I'll see that you get him," he said to the counselor.

Cleanhead opened a card file and fingered through it until he came to the student's card, then rechecked the name and prison number to make sure it was the right person.

"Come on." Cleanhead got up. "Walk me to get this guy from class."

In the hall a guard was hassling a student for not having a pass. The guard was puffed up and loud, but the student held his peace, then turned and went off to get a pass. The guard looked at us but said nothing. We stepped around him and went on.

Cleanhead said, "I'm rehabilitation in action."

I laughed at the unlikely combination of Cleanhead and Dale Carnegie and said, "That's a big switch. Cat burglar to con man."

"It's still burglary," he said. "Only now I'll be climbing into folks' heads to get them to give me what I want, instead of climbing through their windows and taking it."

"A lot safer, too," I added.

He opened the classroom door, stepped inside and gave the teacher the student's name and number, then came out.

"Hell," he said as we walked back toward the office, "I'll always be a burglar."

"No doubt about that," I said.

Big Shorty turned into the hall, waved and came to us.

"Word on the drum has it," Big Shorty said, "that Slick Roland got busted in the Apple again for purse snatching."

"That dude's beyond repair," I said. "He should be hospitalized, not penalized."

"He just needs some D.C.," Cleanhead said.

"What's that?" Big Shorty asked.

"A burglar's disguise," Cleanhead said. We both kept a straight face and left Big Shorty flatfooted in the hallway.

We passed the guard and the student again. This time the student had a pass. He showed it to the guard, then went grinning along the hall.

"By using D.C.," Cleanhead said as we returned to the office, "my M.O. will never be the same."

"How do you figure?"

He sat in his chair and jacked his feet onto the desk. "The only M.O. will be the method of how a victim gives it up, not in how I take it." He was enjoying the logic and took his time breaking it down for me. "No two victims will ever give it up the same way," he said. "So, the M.O. will be different every time."

"Seems to me," I said, "you done found the real deal."

He opened the drawer and said, "You want to see that ad again?"

I thought about it for a moment. "Why not?" I asked. "Everybody here needs a little rehabilitation."

He handed me the ad and said, "Keep it. Pass it on to the next guy."

◆

From here, even the slums look great, fantastic and fine. Steel bars, prowling guards, thick walls between me and my wine.

◆

Narcoticized. We lounged against storefront walls.

Hearing empty baby cry hungry, and our stomachs growl, and tenement rats scurry, even gangster cockroaches seem natural to us.

Until one day.

The storeowner's color TV showed green trees and food and luxuries as real, not myth, and we saw that the pain of living from welfare check to welfare check was not a universal fact.

We smashed the store's window.

Via the pawnshop, we converted the TV into babyfood, three meals a day, rat traps, clothes and rent. In the process we transformed ourselves from a poverty statistic into a self-help program.

◆

Policies and procedures dictate that all prisoners have a work assignment, euphemistically called a "program."

Most assignments are make-work tasks, contributing nothing to rehabilitation, nor preparing a prisoner for eventual release into mainstream society. Yet refusal to accept a meaningless assignment places the prisoner on "idle" status with diminished privileges and limited recreation. Refusal also leaves the prisoner vulnerable for more stringent sanctions and harassment from the guards.

An unprogrammed prisoner is a threat, as dangerous to prison officials as a disobedient slave was to the slavemaster. An example must be made of him before his dissent becomes an example for other prisoners to follow.

An antebellum philosophy permeates the prison walls, and everyone works hard to insure that the charade of full employment is perpetuated.

Old Man Henry Carter

Old Man Henry Carter knew everybody. He had come to prison before rules were rules and no records of him were kept. He didn't even have a number, just a cell, a faded prison uniform, a place in the chow line and a plastic bucket for hot wash water at night.

Old Man Henry's motto was, "You put it out right and it'll come back right." He had a kind word and gentle smile for everyone. Even when young bucks would stomp angrily past his cell and disturb his rest with rabble-rousing shouts, Old Man Henry would smile and quietly remember the years it had taken him to get used to his manhood, too.

The warden created a job for Henry. The warden felt it was important to give Henry a sense that he was earning his keep. Each day Henry swept a clean floor and delivered empty envelopes to people who smiled and called him a "good old boy." And though Old Man Henry never missed a day at work, he would tactfully say that he only worked to ease the warden's guilty conscience.

Two fellow prisoners, members of the Chaplain's Aid Committee, took turns writing so that Old Man Henry would receive some letters at mail call time. They even took turns helping Henry answer their letters so that he would have something going out as well as coming in. Publicly, Old Man Henry would say how nice it was to be in touch with the outside world. But in private, he would wink and thank God that he was able to help the two younger men do their Christian duty.

When Old Man Henry died in his sleep one night, the doctor listed the cause of death as "PRISON." Prisoners walked softly and said no harsh words. Guards laid down their clubs for one day, and the warden ordered steak served in the mess hall.

Andy

Andy was one of the nicest guys in the joint. He was quiet, minded his own business and stayed mostly to himself. That's the criteria for being a good con.

When most prisoners went to the yard for baseball, chess and other recreational games, Andy stayed locked in his cell. He was waiting for his mother to come visit. She never did. Still, he kept his only dress shirt clean and neatly pressed, and he kept his hope alive.

In the yard one Monday morning, Andy spotted a new arrival, a transfer from another prison. He and the new man were not friends, but they came from the same ghetto neighborhood. That's not much, but in prison it is more than enough for an alliance. They greeted each other as "home boy."

Every Sunday, the other man would disappear into the visiting room and on Monday he would tell Andy everything, including the kinds of vending machine sandwiches he and his visitor ate for lunch.

Finally, after some months, Andy confided, "I'm going to have a visit, too. Soon as my mom saves the money to come, she's going to make the trip to the prison and visit me."

Andy repeated this sad line until the other man stopped relating the Monday morning memories of his Sunday visitor. Slowly, the man put a distance between Andy and himself. And when they would chance to come face to face, he would never look Andy in the eyes.

"Did I hurt you in some way?" Andy asked politely. "Why are you avoiding me?"

The man kept his eyes lowered and tactfully tried to evade the truth. Andy pressed for an answer. The man had no choice.

"I feel bad telling you," the man stumbled through his words. "God help me. I can't lie. Your mother isn't coming to visit you. All along, every week, she's been visiting a guy in Cell Block Two. She brings him food and clothes and even puts money into his account."

Andy had stopped listening. Gloom settled over him as if he were the captain of a sinking ship. His mother could visit a man who was locked in a cell not fifty yards away, yet she would not come to see her own son.

The man finished his truth by saying, "I'm sorry to be the one to tell you. Really I am." Then, "God bless you," he said as he walked away.

For the next two weeks Andy didn't speak to anyone, not even to himself. Then one Sunday morning, Andy put on his clean, neatly pressed dress shirt and walked up to a guard. The guard, one of the few humane guards in the prison, greeted Andy with "Good morning." Andy answered by screaming obscenities in the guard's face. The guard tried to recover but Andy didn't give him the chance.

Andy's fist slammed into the guard's face. The second blow took the guard to the floor.

Fellow guards rushed to the rescue. They beat Andy until he begged to die. They left the blood as an example for other prisoners to see before it was mopped away.

The injured guard did not understand and the other guards never asked why Andy had picked him to slug. No one cared; no one wanted to know.

Least of all to care about her son was Andy's mother. She heard the story of his beating on her weekly trip to the prison to visit the other man. The man mentioned it as an afterthought; she received it as conversation in passing.

Doc

Old speckle-haired Doc had more than thirty years behind the wall. He was released on parole only to have his freedom interrupted with an arrest for a crime for which he was
later acquitted and judged not guilty.

But the parole department forced Doc's return to prison
anyway. Guilty or not, the fact that he was arrested is considered a violation of parole. And the law against double jeop-
ardy does not apply.

Junior Rubin

Junior Rubin was a victim of his own making. He
thought he was a tough guy, a butch-kid gangster who could
take whatever he wanted from whomever he wanted. He had
nothing but scorn for those who treated him with respect, and
he used their trust to feed his own narrow needs.

Whenever Junior Rubin was confronted by someone he
had misused, he'd dismiss the complaint with a shrug and
summarily call the person a sucker for trusting him in the first
place.

"If you pet a snake and get bit," Junior laughed, "it's your
fault, not the snake's fault." He said the snake was only following its nature. "Biting the hand that pets it is what any self-
respecting snake would do," Junior smirked, "so why get
pissed at me?" Then he'd walk away and look for someone
else to victimize.

We all learned to stay away from Junior, and word went
around the joint to keep him at arm's length. "Give him all the
space he needs," everybody said. "Feed him with a long
spoon. Let him do his thing—but not on you."

But Little Eduardo didn't see things that way. Eduardo would walk around a problem if he could, but if he couldn't he was more direct than most in dealing with it. When Junior Rubin refused to pay a bet, and added insult by calling Eduardo "a jive-time sucker hick," Little Eduardo stuck a shank between Junior's ribs and twisted the handle to make sure the blade reached Junior's heart.

Junior's self-propaganda promoted him as a tough guy, but his epitaph called him a fool.

Broadway Slim

Broadway Slim claimed to have been a "good doin'" pimp before prison cut short his fast lifestyle. "I had mo' 'hoes on my string than Carter's got Little Liver Pills," he said as he stood near the door to the commissary and tried to con another prisoner out of a Coke.

The spot beside the commissary door was Broadway's late afternoon hustling post. He was always there—as inevitable as a stoplight at a busy street corner—smiling like a cracked dish, forever crying broke and saying he didn't have two of anything. "I ain't got no funds in my account," his mournful voice came like the drone of a black-draped bagpipe. "A lonesome hound dog with a dry bone is doin' better than I is."

Most guys avoided Broadway as they carried their food and snacks from the commissary. The ones who had something to say, usually said "No" to his con, but Broadway was still able to hustle a can or two of Coke and a bag of popcorn each day. On a good day, Broadway got an ice cream sandwich too.

Whenever we needed a prime example of a physically

ruined human being, we always invoked Broadway's name: He stammered when he talked and when he got excited a fine mist sprayed out with his words. To conceal the wide bald spot in the middle of his Afro, he wore his hat cocked on the side of his head; his nose was pushed in and one eye, larger than the other, resembled a gleaming hubcap in an auto wreck.

His legs, ankles and feet had been badly broken. When he walked, his thighs pinched in, rubbing his knobby knees together. Standing still, his long legs slanted out, away from his lanky body like the sides of the letter "A." His ankles were twisted and his flat feet formed awkward angles as if trying to walk away from each other.

Still, he had a good—and sometimes strange—sense of humor and, more than the rest of us, he knew that no one ever took him seriously.

Most of us who listened to Broadway's colorful accounts of pandering, as a highflying, flamboyant pimp, dismissed his tales as wishful thinking—sap-rap that was nothing more than Broadway's daily recreation program and a major component of his prison image. To us, his stories were handy debris, a kind of landfill that kept us from having too many empty spaces in our days. We urged him on, and often helped him fill in the details, but we suspected he had lived a hand-to-mouth existence and that the only women who ever willingly put their bodies in his hands were a few street hags and one or two bag ladies.

But we never challenged the truth of Broadway's stories, nor did we ever call him a liar. Our code didn't permit that. In prison, histories are created on the spot. Men who couldn't pay fifty-dollars for bail swore they'd been million-dollar drug dealers who owned a fleet of limos. Everybody's holster was embroidered with fringes. No one was willing to hear the truth about himself in retaliation for telling the truth about another man's lies. For us, Broadway's tales were just an ordinary part of doing our time.

Although Broadway talked about everything else— much of which he knew nothing about—he never talked about the "accident" which broke his lower limbs. That was taboo, and whenever we'd try questioning him, he'd stammer, "T'ain't none of your business, so don't even try it." With that he'd cut the conversation short.

But his refusal to talk didn't stop us from talking. Some speculated, some gossiped and a few claimed to know the facts, but most of us talked because we had lips and didn't have anything better to do with them.

Our favorite story, and therefore the one repeated as true, had Broadway being forced—at gun point—to jump from a fourth-floor window of a rundown Times Square hotel. His legs, feet and ankles were smashed when he hit the concrete sidewalk below. The doctor set the bones as best he could, but too many had been crushed to allow the limbs to mend correctly.

According to this story, the two brothers of a young woman Broadway had kidnapped kicked their way into his hotel room and cornered him in a closet. Broadway had drugged the woman and tried to force her into prostitution. Her brothers were two of Harlem's meanest. They wore death on their faces like a plague; each was tough enough to kiss cactus, and rumor had it they had enough kills to fill a private graveyard.

They took one look at their kid sister and without saying a word cocked the hammers on their sawed-off shotguns and gave Broadway a choice: jump out the window or take the full blast in his face.

A point-blank shotgun blast was certain death, a jump

from a fourth-floor window was a maybe.

Broadway Slim jumped.

The brothers never expected Broadway to survive the plunge, but Broadway crawled away, trailing a stream of blood along the sidewalk. New Yorkers took the sight in stride, stepped around him and went on about their business. Even while the doctor was still patching him up, Broadway was confessing the kidnapping to the cops. At first chance, he pled guilty to the charges and begged the judge to sentence him to prison. For Broadway, being in prison was a better option than being hunted down by the woman's shotgun-wielding brothers.

Broadway conned a Coke from a guy who'd just come from the commissary, and then he turned and started to work Cold Duck for a box of Fig Newtons.

Cold Duck held the cookies in front of Broadway like bait. "These sure are good," Cold Duck said as he shook the box, rattling the cookies around inside. "They're the greatest eat in the world. 'Specially with some ice-cold milk."

Cold Duck had Broadway Slim drooling.

"That's right man," Broadway stammered, sending out a mist of spit. "Fig cookies and milk, that's just what I had in mind." He reached an anxious hand for the cookies. "I got me a whole quart of cold milk stashed in my cell. Fresh from the mess hall. Milk just waiting to meet these cookies."

As Broadway's finger touched the box, Cold Duck yanked it away, out of Broadway's reach.

"Not so fast," Cold Duck grinned. Playful sadism marked his face.

"Don't worry," Broadway continued his con, "I'm'a pay you back as soon as I get my account straightened out."

"You never paid back before."

"You can bank on what I say," Broadway's words dripped with con. "My word is gold."

"Fool's gold," Cold Duck laughed and turned the conversation back to the cookies in his hand. "Now Broadway, before I give up my Fig Newtons, I want a small favor."

"Name it." Broadway could already taste the cookies in his mouth. "You and me is as close as white on rice. Ain't no favor too much for you." His fingers were octopus tentacles, inching closer to the box of cookies. "What's the favor you want?"

"Tell me," Cold Duck dropped his bombshell on Broadway, "what happened to your legs?"

Broadway stopped reaching for the cookies. His hand dropped to his side and he pulled his shoulder back.

"You want my cookies, don't you?" Cold Duck said. "A fair exchange ain't robbery."

"What you doing is lowdown and funky-foul." Broadway had an angry scowl on his face. "So don't even try it with me."

"But..."

Broadway spun around and walked away. After that he never tried his con on Cold Duck again. Not even when Cold Duck offered something for nothing in return would Broadway take it.

Hard Luck Henry

We watched Hard Luck Henry being led away across the yard by four guards. He'd just gotten busted for drinking jailhouse booze in the baseball dugout and they were taking him to the Hole.

"I've known Hard Luck for a long, long, time," Little

Brother T said. "We go way back together. We were once running partners on the street, and it don't surprise me one bit
that he got flagged with wine on his breath. That's one dude
that's always into something or other. One time he called me
at three o'clock in the morning from a pay phone booth and
says that he's in a jam and wants me to hurry over and pick
him up. When I got on the scene he was in the phone booth,
buck-ass naked. He had one shoe on, and his hat in his hand.
He said he was screwing some woman and her husband came
home and he had to jump out the window and run."

We all laughed.

"You know something?" Little Brother T said with a
straight face. "I never did ask him where he got the dimes for
the phone call."

Inside History

**It is a poor spider
that builds its web
in the corner of my cell.**

Sparrow

"HEY, BROTHER," Sparrow called Demon to a halt. "I need some info."

"Sure thing," Demon said, always willing to rap. "What'll it be?"

"When a woman wants to give a man some money," Sparrow said awkwardly, somewhat embarrassed, "how do you take it gracefully."

"You mean, how do you get the money," Demon clarified the question, "and not make it seem like you're playing games on her?"

"Yeah. Exactly."

"Well," Demon picked his words like a chicken feeding in a rocky yard. "You just let her know that normally you wouldn't be broke, but the prison situation done got you down and doing bad and has forced you to come to her for temporary relief."

Sparrow thought it over, then asked, "Is that it?"

Demon said, "One more thing."

"What?"

"Make sure that she understands to give you all she can get."

Sparrow thought it over again, thanked Demon for the help, then strutted across the prison yard to where Miss Joy, a grey-haired, wrinkle-faced homo lounged against the wall.

Junior Wise

A bunch of the boys were rappin' around a table in the exercise yard. Some were spreading rumors and gossip, slick-talk and jive, while others told outright lies. Pittsburgh Bob topped a tale by Eddie Too-Fast and had the group laughing in guffaws, like children at a clown show, when Junior Wise stopped everybody cold.

Junior, one of the youngest in the joint, was the newest member of the group. He'd come to prison fresh out of high school biology class, where, high on Angel Dust, he tried to dissect the teacher instead of the dead frog. Although he was big for his age, youth and inexperience put an awkward edge on his voice. It crackled like static from a bargain-basement radio.

"Once," Junior said proudly, "I had the clap." As an afterthought, he added, "At least I think I did."

"Shee-it!" Pittsburgh Bob slurred his words around the filter-tipped cigarette clamped between his front teeth. "Man," he said, "either you had the clap, or you ain't had it. There ain't no thinking about it, because the clap don't let you think."

"That's right," Eddie Too-Fast put in before Junior could respond: "When you got it, you sure as hell gonna know it. There just ain't no two ways about it."

"Especially when the third day rolls around," Pittsburgh Bob went on, "because as soon as you try to piss, that old clap is gonna have you hunting for some penicillin."

"And in a hurry, too," another voice said.

Junior was learning what high-school sex education never taught him.

Eddie chimed in again, "Man, your nuts will be burning like you're trying to piss fire, and you'll be running to the doctor faster than a junkie needing a fix."

"I really thought I had the clap," Junior muttered. He was as confused as a pup with a rubber bone. "Now I'm not too sure."

"Well, son," Pittsburgh Bob draped a lanky arm across the younger man's shoulder. Pittsburgh's face was as straight as a nun's petticoat. "First of all, have you ever had a woman?"

"What does that have to do with the clap?" Junior's words were out of his mouth and being laughed at by the others before he realized he had said them.

From then on, Junior Wise was accepted as one of the boys, and he was well on his way to being recognized as a legendary liar.

Jivin' Jimmy Green

Jivin' Jimmy Green is wrapped in razzmatazz and litanies of bullshit! He once played Harlem's famed Apollo Theater. Sang and sand-danced until the audience, tired of laughing at him, turned nasty with boos, and somebody reached a shepherd's hook from backstage and snatched his narrow ass out of the spotlight. Not even an echo of his song was left to linger on the stage where Jivin' Jimmy once stood.

Fast nightlife and petty drug deals put him in prison. Now he stars every afternoon with the doo-wop crowd stationed in a dismal corner of the exercise yard.

Jivin' Jimmy Green is cool!

◆

Polite guys are never rude. They'll always say, "Excuse me" before burying a knife in another man's chest.

The Blues Merchant

Long Tongue, The Blues Merchant, strolls on stage. His guitar rides sidesaddle against his hip. The drummer slides onto the tripod seat behind the drums, adjusts the high-hat cymbal, and runs a quick, off-beat tattoo on the tom-tom, then relaxes. The bass player plugs into the amplifier, checks the settings on the control panel and nods his okay. Three horn players stand off to one side, clustered, lurking like brilliant sorcerer-wizards waiting to do magic with their musical instruments.

The auditorium is packed. A thousand inmates face the stage; all anticipate a few minutes of musical escape. The tear gas canisters recessed in the ceiling remind us that everything is for real.

The house lights go down and the stage lights come up. Reds and greens and blues slide into pinks and ambers and yellows and play over the six poised musicians.

The Blues Merchant leans forward and mumbles, "Listen. Listen here, you all," into the microphone. "I want to tell you about Fancy Foxy Brown and Mean Lean Green. They is the slickest couple in the East Coast scene."

Thump. Thump. The drummer plays. Boom-chicka-chicka-boom. He slams his tubs. The show is on. Toes tap. Hands clap. Fingers pop. The audience vibrates. Long Tongue finds his groove. He leans back. He moans. He shouts. His message is picked up, translated and understood. With his soul he releases us from bondage, puts us in tune with tomorrow, and the memories of the cold steel cells—our iron houses—evaporate.

Off to one side, a blue coated guard nods to the rhythm. On the up-beat his eyes meet the guard sergeant's frown. The message is clear: "You are not supposed to enjoy the blues.

You get paid to watch, not be human." The message is instantaneously received. The guard jerks himself still and looks meaner than ever.

Long Tongue, The Blues Merchant, wails on. He gets funky. He gets rough. He gets raunchy. His blues are primeval. He takes everybody, except the guards, on a trip. The guards remain trapped behind the prison's walls while, if only for a short time, we are free.

The blues is our antidote, and Long Tongue, The Blues Merchant, is our doctor.

♦

We stood in the cold exercise yard, ankle deep in snow and watched a televised movie. Most of the men cheered for the TV cops. I thought they were pathetic and was about to voice my opinion when someone whispered a warning.

"The warden is watching us," the voice said.

After that I cheered the TV cops, too.

Pop Rivers

Throughout the winter Pop Rivers spread bread crumbs for the pigeons. He found one sick and nursed it back to health. By spring the bird could have flown away; instead it followed Pop around the yard. Pop named the pigeon Henry and referred to it as his child. He fed Henry a special mixture of cereal, cookie crumbs and crushed potato chips. Sometimes Pop would give Henry a spoon of sugar, at other times a drink of milk. But Henry's favorite food was popcorn.

At night when Pop Rivers had to be locked in his cell, he'd put Henry in a cardboard box on a table in the yard. Pop always left the box open and Henry was free to leave, but

Pop's cell was never left open. In the morning when Pop came out for his walk, Henry was always there.

When Pop came out on the morning of the summer solstice, Henry was not in his box. He was on the table. The bird's head had been chopped off, his wings and legs severed from the body, and Henry's heart had been cut out. All the parts had been arranged in a neat line and the blood was still sticky.

Pop Rivers and a few friends went to the guard captain and pleaded that an investigation be made. "Who murdered Henry while we inmates slept locked safely in our cells?" Pop cried.

"We don't plan to investigate," the captain snapped. "But if you insist, I'll give you thirty days in the Hole for violating the rules against having a pet in the first place."

Pop Rivers could do nothing but silently curse the captain and find a place for Henry's grave.

The Soap Opera

All winter Dobbson sat in the South Yard watching his favorite TV soap opera. On the coldest days, Dobbson was there, bundled like an Eskimo, drinking hot coffee from his half-gallon thermos, clapping his mittened hands and stomping his feet to keep the blood flowing. Even when the snow blew in ten-foot drifts against the wall, Dobbson was there.

Many times Dobbson would be the only inmate out in the freezing yard and the shivering guard sergeant would plead for him to go inside. But Dobbson would just shake his head and say, "No good. This is my recreation and I'm going to enjoy myself." As long as Dobbson stayed in the yard, a full guard complement also had to stay out. The guards suffered, but Dobbson didn't. He watched his soap opera and forgot about the cold.

When spring came Dobbson was joined by other inmates. They were often loud and sometimes inconsiderate. They didn't really care for the soap opera and were only watching because they had no place else to be. But that didn't bother Dobbson. He was intent on his soap opera and paid them little attention. He had spent all winter with his soap opera and now that it was spring, he was in love and his world didn't include other inmates.

Dobbson's love wasn't the painful kind that people fall into and out of as if it were a container. It was a liberating love that offered a fantastic escape, and left him with a gratifying taste on his lips.

One sunny afternoon a couple of guys were high-jiving nearby, and one commented as he watched the female star of Dobbson's soap opera strut across the video screen, "Man," he said, "that there broad sure is a fine looking bitch."

Dobbson stiffened, but said nothing.

"Bet she can handle a joint like a flat-back whore at a cut-rate fire sale," the other guy said.

The first agreed. "A bitch like that," he said, "can cannibalize a swipe with one move."

Dobbson turned, looked at the two with cold eyes and said, "You men have got to show folks respect."

"Respect? Who? What?"

"The lady on TV," Dobbson said.

"Man, are you crazy?"

The other said, "That bitch is a thousand miles away and if she was right here, she wouldn't be worth my respect."

"You had better cool your roles," Dobbson warned. "Don't oversport your hands."

"I can always play my hand," one of the two wolfed,

"and I know a two-bit bitch when I see one. And that there *is* one." He pointed to the soap opera's star.

"She ain't no bitch," Dobbson said. His eyes narrowed to a squint as he sized up the two men. "She's my woman."

Both guys laughed, but Dobbson didn't crack a smile. This wasn't a laughing matter. He got up and quietly walked away.

When they saw Dobbson returning, they started to laugh again, but they didn't see the steel pipe that Dobbson carried low against his right hip. When they did see it, it was too late to run or even defend themselves. Dobbson struck. Blood, scalp and hair flew. Two bodies caved to the ground.

"Those guys have got to learn to respect another man's woman," Dobbson said as the guards rushed him away. "They have *got* to learn respect."

Mackin' Mo

"Man, you've got a game for them all," Slim Sam said to slick-talking Mackin' Mo.

Mackin' Mo, coming on slick out of the side of his mouth, said, "Nowdays, I'm looking for a ninety year old woman. One that can't walk. She ain't got to come visit. All she's got to do is sit in her wheelchair and write the checks."

"That's what I call real strong game," Slim Sam praised him.

"The old rugged cross was more humane than I am," Mackin' Mo quipped as he watched two homos pass and wondered how he could exploit their talents.

◆

Each day I feed the birds outside my window. Since I am never sure if today's birds are the same as yesterday's, I limit my conversation to a few "hello's" and a casual, "Hi there."

Extended conversations are impossible when no continuum can be identified.

Still, each day the birds come to pimp me for bread. And each day I pimp them for companionship. We pimp each other for survival.

Isn't that also a law of nature?

Dixie and Sweet Meat

Dixie was a first-class freak, as kinky as they come. No man was hung too large for Dixie, and none was too small. Size was never a problem, and he was always prepared. He never wore undershorts, carried a tube of Vaseline in his hip pocket and had a nice set of teeth that he soaked in a jar of solution overnight.

While Dixie enjoyed a reputation for being good, quick and giving the hottest head in the joint, he also had a reputation for being selective. Only a fool who couldn't find a high place to leap from, or some other way of committing suicide, would dare try to force Dixie into sex. But prison is filled with fools. They come in all shapes, sizes, and sexual persuasions. Most fools are known, but some are camouflaged and hard to spot. Still they are as inescapable as the reflection from a full-length mirror. While Dixie's reputation was ubiquitous, it was not fool-proof.

One Sunday morning when almost everyone else was at breakfast, a fool who called himself Sweet Meat eased up to the front of Dixie's pink cell and demanded a quick face-job.

Dixie was cool. He held his anger in check and gave

Sweet Meat a seductive yet deceptive smile. "Sure," Dixie responded. His voice was a soft falsetto. "I'd love to." Dixie laid aside the women's fashion magazine he'd been reading. "Unzip," Dixie whispered as he came to the front of his locked cell and knelt on the floor, "Just stick it in through the bars to me."

Sweet Meat checked in both directions to make sure no one was watching. Then he pressed his stomach against the cell bars, thrust his narrow hips forward and poked his erection into the cell toward Dixie's open mouth.

Without warning or the slightest hesitation, Dixie whipped out a prison-issued double-edged razor blade. Before Sweet Meat could scream in terror or beg Dixie's mercy, Dixie sliced the length of Sweet Meat's cock, splitting it down the middle from tip to root, like a log laid raw by a lumberjack's ax.

Orangutan Jones

The first sign that Orangutan Jones was losing his grip came when he removed his woman's photo from the wall of his cell. It was an eight-by-ten, full-color blowup from a snapshot of a good time they had once on a North Shore beach. She had it especially made into a calendar and had written on it: "With each day you mark off, we'll be coming closer together. All my love, until the end." She had written that last year and the end came shortly thereafter.

Orangutan Jones treasured that photo and often stated that it brought good memories. "Sometimes," he said, "when I look at it, I forget that I'm here in prison at all." Now it was gone from his wall and only the gummy marks of the tape which had held it there remained.

"It's the small things that get to me," Orangutan said as we walked the exercise yard. "Bit by bit, like Chinese water torture. At first I told myself not to take it personal." He ripped up the photo and a number of her letters—the latest was five months old—and dropped them into a trash can. "All it takes is a small show of love and a little reassurance from the outside for a guy to make it in here, and she couldn't even give that. A lie would have been better than the nothing she gave."

Three days later the guards found him sitting in the middle of the basketball court. He was bouncing a ball, crying and babbling to himself. They thought it was delirium brought on by jailhouse booze, but to me the meaning was clear.

That night I lay awake re-hearing Orangutan Jones as he was led to the observation room. "I want to thank you, baby," he said, "for all the little things you didn't do for me."

When dawn came, I was still wondering if I'd be the next to say those words.

Lobo

Lobo, a bad motherhumper outta Biloxi, planted an icepick in Turner's skull and stood by the body until the guards came to drag him away.

Redneck guards, who always hide their killings and other wrongs behind walls of lies, couldn't understand why Lobo didn't try to run away.

"Damn, you is stupid," Lobo said in his thick southern drawl. "Dis is yo' prison 'n you don't even know there ain't no place to run?"

♦

My history is my cross. A dead weight. The mathemati-
cal certainties of one-plus-one, two-times-two, have more
flexibility.

A gravestone might state arrival, departure, the date-
time group, and an occasional epitaph of atonement or wit.

But my history lives.

It crawls. It slouches. It slurps. It marches and dances
and laughs and shouts. It trembles and treads. Runs. It is a
child and can fly.

Sometimes my history stomps angrily in the vanguard,
directing the patterns my future will take. More often it is
quiet, dormant; my history lurks behind this circus clown's
face where I live.

Old Gates

Over the years, Old Gates had lost his teeth. The state replaced them with ever-white porcelain ones. They worked
well enough but were not the same as the real thing.

Most of his hair had fallen out and the little he had left
had turned grey. The steel walls of the cell had sapped his
strength, the poor lighting had weakened his eyesight. The
cheap mattress had curved his back and he limped on knees
smashed by a guard's club. He hadn't had a visitor in eleven
years and his only mail was a monthly religious magazine and
an occasional throwaway because someone had forgotten to
remove his name from an ancient mailing list.

Old Gates was senior man in the license plate shop
where we stamped out plates for models of cars he'd never
seen. He never asked anyone for anything and when he went
to the yard he sat alone. Long ago, Old Gates stopped looking
at the sky, envying the birds their freedom. Now all he saw

was their droppings. It blighted the yard and he worried about it falling on him.

One night, sick in his cell, Old Gates asked for a doctor. The guard told him that no doctor was on duty at that hour, that he'd have to hang on until morning. But Old Gates was tired of hanging on. He laid down and never got up.

During the morning head count the guard found Old Gates cold and still and never having to worry about bird shit again.

♦

"This won't take long," Captain Boss of the blue shirt mob said. "It'll be over and done with long before you know, or even suspect, what we'll be doing is happening to you." He smiled like a part-time friend. "Don't fight back," he said, "or you'll break my club."

♦

Next to the flagpole, in front of Attica Prison, is a granite monument. On the monument, in alphabetical order, are the names of the eleven civilians and prison guards who were slaughtered in the riot of '71. They were picked off by their fellow guards, co-workers, Attica neighbors, and lifelong friends when Rockefeller ordered the prison yard to be retaken. The monument symbolizes the collective guilt shared by the living.

Forty-three were killed that day. But, as if no prisoners ever lived, therefore never died, none of the dead prisoners' names are memorialized in granite.

Each morning, a trusted prisoner strolls out to raise the flag. Each evening, he returns to lower the flag. In between, he sits in his cell. In between, he does not exist.

Juanito: The Song of Life

And the guards storm the yard sixty strong. They come four abreast. Shoulder to shoulder. Sweat drips from their red necks like spit from a jackal's jaw. They refuse a one-to-one, man-to-man fight. They are heroes in a mob—a mob of heroes.

Their tear gas rolls on us like fog covering a seafront. We retreat, coughing and gagging on our vomit, against the prison wall. We cover our heads with folded arms to protect them against their clubs and pickax handles. And even those prisoners not involved are dragged by their heels and beaten until their blood refuses to flow—until blood refused to flow.

Only quiet little Juanito stands his ground. He shouts, a breeze against the hurricane. *"Better it is to die in laughter than in tears to live."*

Nine months later we are released from the Hole. The bread and water, oatmeal and salted coffee we were fed twice a day are behind us. Now our stomachs will not hold down solid food. Our eyes are weak and burn in the light. After the Hole, our legs ache from lack of exercise.

It is then we hear how the jackals pulled Juanito from his cell, stripped him naked and dragged him to torture him in private, crowding around like buzzards drawn to carrion—the dead meat of American justice.

And we hear how the head jackal put his nightstick across Juanito's throat, and the point of his knee against Juanito's spine. And how the head jackal yanked until Juanito's neck snapped like a fragile crystal wand caught in a vise.

And the other jackals—caricatures of men—cheered and stamped their jackboots onto quiet little Juanito's twisted body. And called Juanito "Spic" and stamped until Juanito's ribs caved in. The boots that kicked after that only moved the broken parts around.

And we hear how the head jackal drove twenty-five miles to find a doctor who signed the death certificate and swore that Juanito hanged himself. The prison doctor, sober for once, refused to be a part of that lie.

And we hear how Juanito, enduring his ground, laughed. And his laugh made proud the ghosts of his forefathers who rode to the end with Zapata, and laughed to the end with Zapata, and passed that laugh—the song of life—on to Juanito.

And we ask our forefathers to forgive us as we hear Juanito's voice crowned with yesterday's blood calling across time into this dead place, urging us to laugh in the jackal's face, not live with tears in our hearts.

And while we know that Juanito was right to die laughing, our fears conjure us to stand in our cells and have our heads counted like empty bottles on a Coca-Cola production line.

Saladine

When Saladine refused to take Thorazine, the guards said that he was rebelling. When Saladine tightened his fist against the pain of fifteen years in prison, the guards said that he had given the Black Power salute. When Saladine went to the parole board and asked to be released, the guards labeled him a "malcontent." When Saladine exploded and sent three fellow prisoners to the hospital, the guards relaxed and called Saladine a "well-adjusted prisoner."

Lame Jones

"You would do better picking your victims with more care," the doctor suggested as he stitched the gash in Lame Jones' head. "This is the third time in two months that your plots have backfired and sent you to the hospital."

"Yes, sir." Lame grimaced against the pain in his head. "I'll change my approach."

"Good idea." The doctor tied off the last stitch, swabbed away a trickle of oozing blood and taped on a bandage. "I can't keep reporting that you injured yourself falling out of bed."

"Yes, sir," Lame Jones agreed, "Somebody might get suspicious."

"Either that," the doctor said, "or you're going to get yourself killed."

Hardrock

"You ain't playing wid no kids in the park," Hardrock yelled as he bashed the guard sergeant in the face, "This is ME! Hardrock! I got my manhood to preserve."

The guard sergeant backpedaled and called out a goon squad of guards.

Outnumbered three to one, Hardrock fought a courageous but futile battle. They rumbled through a corridor, past Cellblock D, wrestled in front of the chapel door, and came to a standstill at the mess hall gate.

The guards backed Hardrock into a supply room and cornered him against the back wall. Hardrock ducked, bobbed and dodged like a prize fighter on the ropes. For every blow the guards managed to land, Hardrock returned two.

Stinging jabs, left hooks, short rights and uppercuts held the guards at bay.

Reinforcements arrived and still Hardrock stood toe-to-toe. A fair referee would have stopped the fight and called it a draw, but the sergeant's image was at stake and fairness didn't get a play. The final outcome was decided by the force of the guards' clubs and confirmed by the blood Hardrock left to stain the supply room floor.

Even though he was hospitalized and charged with assault, it was Hardrock, not the sergeant, whom everybody hailed as the winner. Hardrock had stood and fought with bare fists to preserve his manhood; the sergeant stood to one side and let the goon squad preserve his.

Nobody's Hoss

Bo Green came to Attica in a snowstorm. Everybody else was chained together in teams of two, but Bo Green was chained to himself. His hands were cuffed and the steel cuffs were padlocked to a heavy link chain locked around his waist. His ankles were shackled like hobbles on a horse, and the ankle chain dragged as he climbed down from the prison bus and shuffled in through the door to the reception hall.

Bo Green's hair was wild and napped in kinks; he had a head cold and his temperature was running high. His eyes were red from the cold and the handcuffs locked to the chain around his waist prevented him from wiping his dripping nose. Snot caked his bushy mustache and was dried in streaks down the front of his prison coat. He was tired and hungry from riding the bus all day and he wasn't in the mood to be friendly.

A beefy-faced hack named Wilson made the mistake of

singling out Bo as an example. "Pick the meanest looking one in the bunch," Wilson said, instructing the new-jack rookie guards on how to establish authority when receiving new prisoners. "Get right in his face," he said, "and lean on him. Hard!"

To demonstrate his technique, Wilson slapped his nightstick against the palm of his hand and barked in Bo's face. "This here is Attica prison, boy. This is the last stop before your grave. You're my hoss, and I'm your boss. What *I* say is law. Got that, boy?"

Wilson stood by grinning, self-satisfied, assured, while another guard removed Bo Green's handcuffs and shackles. Then to prove that his authority was absolute, Wilson slapped his stick against the palm of his hand again, and leaned forward to bark into Bo's face once more.

But leaning forward was as far as Wilson ever got. Bo Green's hands were free and his thick body was square as a concrete block. His left jab jammed the words back down into Wilson's throat. Wilson's lips twisted out of shape, his head snapped back; his eyes were as wide with surprise as a mugger mugged on his own home turf. He raised his nightstick to make a feeble defense, and looked around for room to run. Bo Green's lashing right cross smashed Wilson's nose, splitting open his upper lip. A short left hook broke Wilson's jaw and drove his out-of-shape body to the floor. "This hoss can kick!" Bo Green shouted over and over as he stomped Wilson's chest.

Four guards pounced on Bo, two more dragged Wilson away. Bo Green fought until his back was to the wall, where they beat him bloody and clubbed him to the floor.

Years later when Bo Green was let out of solitary, he was blind in one eye and walked with a limp. His brace of beautiful white teeth had been broken from the gums, and nerve damage caused his right hand to twitch. The guards' revenge had weakened his body and aged him before his time.

Now he just wanders sort of aimlessly around the yard, and sometimes he sits in the sun. Once in a while he mutters, "I ain't nobody's hoss. Ain't never been, and ain't never will." But he never says much of anything else.

The guards give him plenty of room, and for a while a few of the older prisoners who still remembered would point Bo out. But mostly everyone else has forgotten about the fight, and some of the younger men, new to Attica, refuse to believe it happened at all.

Dusty Moore

Dusty Moore had bowed, bandy legs. Rickets when he was a kid. He ate plaster in a slum and swallowed paint until chunks of red lead slowed his brain to a stumble. He talked to God—no one else would listen—and what he said put a dirge in our hearts. Still, Dusty's smile was as open as a church, and he hugged his thin future like a lover carrying roses.

He came to prison after making headlines for robbery and he died two years later from gunshot wounds while trying to escape.

We built a monument for Dusty. A smashed garbage can, gnarled and wrapped around a shithouse steampipe. We didn't put his name on the monument. The warden would have ordered it ripped down. We're allowed to praise the Lord, not a home-grown hero. Especially not one who died while attempting to escape. Even the guards know, yet don't say anything. Dusty's memory gives them strength to get through their days in prison, too.

♦

"It's not possible for you to be feeling that much pain," the prison doctor said, leaning back in his chair and frowning up at me.

"I hurt all over," I said, "My stomach is burning up. I want you to do something for me."

"Give this man a handkerchief," he said to his nurse. Then to me, "Wipe your tears before they drip on my magazine and soil the playmate's navel."

Pious Pete

"If you want to learn to crack a safe," the education officer said, "ask Pious Pete."

Pious Pete is the chaplain's inmate clerk. He looks two days older than water and has more time on the toilet than I have in prison. His record as a safe-cracker is listed in fifteen states and two territories.

"Old Pete knows everything there is to know about cracking a safe," the officer said, then added, "but after pulling a job, he just doesn't know how to get away."

I thanked him for the information, turned and started off.

"Remember," he calls after me, "there ain't no get-away experts in prison. For that," he laughs, "best bet is to do a Richard Nixon."

I made a mental note to do that and went off in search of Pious Pete.

♦

They told me that I was sent to Attica for "re-programming." When I arrived, shackled and chained and begging to get involved, the KKK, operating under the banner of the guards' union, laid a just-hung Puerto Rican boy on the floor. They said he had died from "hyperactivity."

And the guards made jokes about how the boy's choked-swollen tongue propped open his jaw "like a just-boiled hog." They even refused to allow a white prisoner to close the Rican's dead eyes.

On Sunday, the reverend who sang "Mammy" while King led marches, refused to pray for the dead boy's soul. He claimed the warden feared a riot if the Puerto Rican's memory was dignified with prayer.

And the dead Rican's mother could not understand that reprogramming at Attica, when translated into Spanish, means to cut off your own balls and hand them to the Man, smile and say, "Thank you, sir, for trusting me with your knife."

Food for Thought

We laughed and jived and bullshitted all the way to the mess hall.

Our guards thought that with the lure of overcooked rib steak and mashed potatoes our spirits had finally been broken—that we had forgotten what had happened at Attica.

When we got into the mess hall, we didn't eat; we didn't talk. Our jive and bullshit had been checked at the door and our laughter transformed into a silent indictment. The guards stood in their dishonest boots and twitched in their skins of guilt while we breathed a common breath and lowered our eyes and remembered our history.

Then we laughed and jived and bullshitted all the way back to our cells.

♦

The shrink's first question always is: "Are you sure that you want to be 'sane'?"

I give it some thought, bounce the idea off the prison wall, weigh the possibilities and answer, "No."

The shrink smiles like a glutton feasting on gourmet cuisine. He stamps my file "Unadjusted" and adds my name to the "pay-him-no-mind" list.

The guards hold their clubs at the ready and fellow prisoners whisper behind my back. Everyone stands aside. Even certified bona fide killers lower their eyes when I pass.

Pete Moss

"Yo, man," Pete Moss called out from the cell next to mine. "Anybody got any of that scientific milk?"

"Huh?" Eighty odd voices shouted back. "What the fuck is 'scientific milk'?"

The few who didn't shout, laughed.

"You know, that powdered stuff," Pete Moss shouted again, "that shit what you put in coffee."

Everyone fell quiet as if trying to decipher a code.

I found the answer. "Coffee creamer," I called back to Pete Moss. "*Synthetic milk?*" I asked. "Is that what you want?"

"Yeah, that's it." Pete Moss didn't miss a beat. "That's what I said. Scientific milk!"

I kept my mouth shut as I passed the creamer out through my cell bars and handed it to Pete Moss in the next cell. "Scientific milk," I thought, "My God, what a dastardly *cor-rip-shen of the languish.*"

◆

"This used to be a good joint," the electric gate guard said.

They had taken his keys and refitted him with push button controls. The buttons were color coded so he wouldn't confuse the word "open" with "close" and let a prisoner go free.

"Back in the old days when Lefty Collins was a tough guy, and Shorty Dog would fight back, we had a *real good* place here." He emphasized "real good," then lamented, "now I almost feel shame when we gang up on one of these new-breed prisoners. They worry more about bouncing a basket-ball than keeping their manhood."

He pushed his buttons and remembered the simplicity of turning a key and said, "It just ain't no fun kicking a pacified ass."

◆

"So what if this food is unfit for canine consumption?" the Mess Sargeant said. "We ain't feeding dogs, we is feeding you." He gloated, then added, "The SPCA can't squawk about that."

Crapgame

"If you ever want to run a heavy con game on a victim," Crapgame explained, "you first have to let the vic think he's got the upper hand. When you've got him all fixed—mesmer-ized—he'll con himself. Then all you've got to do is lay in the cut, and count his bucks."

Leapfrog

Leapfrog, standing in the chow line behind K.C. Lou, watched the food server flop sliced ham onto the trays of the inmates in front of them.

"Swine is bad for your health," Leapfrog said to K.C. Lou.

"No shit," said K.C., as the line moved one step forward.

"Sure," Leapfrog said. "The pig is a grafted animal. The cat-rat-dog. Scavenges its own shit. The abomination of all abominations. Save your life, don't eat the ham." He paused, then said, "Best thing to do is to give yours to me."

"Fuck you," K.C. Lou retorted: "Swine is divine; it's boss with hot sauce."

♦

At noon today we waited an extra half hour to get into the mess hall. It was so nice to be free from the steel cells that, at first, no one minded the wait. There was a lot of bullshit-ting, joking, sap-rapping and high-jiving—the kinds of trivia inmates get into to relieve the tension.

Then the rumors started. They came like birds in the night, and no one could pinpoint their origin.

The first rumor attributed the delay to Muslim inmates in the mess crew. The scheduled meal was ham, and to Mus-lims even handling swine is a sin, so they were refusing to serve it; in turn, they would save us from ourselves. The word rushed from mouth to ear to mouth; like falling dominoes the rumor went through the chow line. Before the word had reached the terminal of the last ear, a new message was on the drum.

Now the rumor spread that a rat had been found stewing in the wax beans, and for the vegetarians, this is a no-no. Next it came that soap powder had been used instead of cornstarch to thicken the gravy. Another told of a mouse committing suicide in the chocolate pudding. Each rumor sounded truer than the one before. They were all conceivable. We had little doubt that, in that kitchen, anything could happen.

Soon, like echoes, angry gripes followed the stream of rumors; the wake was alive with whispers of militant flotsam.

A nervous guard picked up the growing vexation, and finally a guard sergeant showed on the scene. Awkwardly, he explained that health inspectors were touring the mess hall and that chow was being delayed until after their inspection.

We had no more reason to believe him than the other things we had heard. Yet when we did get to eat, it was with the feeling that, for once, it was safe.

Tale of Two Foxes

"Yo, homey, whatcha got to munch on?" Little Black asked as he bounced to a halt in front of Berry's cell. Little Black was hyperactive and always seemed to be in a hurry.

"I'm doing bad." Berry laid his newspaper on the bed next to where he sat. "B-A-D," he spelled the word, emphasizing each letter with the corners of his lips turned down.

"Save that crap for somebody who don't know any better," Little Black said. "You ain't never doing bad."

"Word up," Berry said, "ain't nothing in my locker except a can of jive o' tuna fish."

Little Black and Berry had been locking in cells close to each other for nearly three years. Before that they knew each other for another five years in and around most of the maximum security prisons across the state. Little Black was serving ten-to-fifteen for armed robbery. His specialty had been

New York City subway token booths. Berry had been a cat burglar, sneaking across roof tops at night, and lowering himself into apartment windows. Each thought the other's crimes were crazy things to do, but in prison they were hustling buddies, and at times they even hustled each other.

"Tuna? That's all?" Little Black was disappointed. "I'm hungry as a lobo wolf and I need something to snack on."

"I'll give up my tuna," Berry started negotiating a deal, "if you'll mix up a salad and put me down with a sandwich."

"That's a bet," Little Black said. "Break out the tuna."

They sealed their deal with a slap of hands—a gesture more binding than a court sanctioned contract.

Berry reached into his food locker and came out of the cell with the can of tuna. "Do you have onions and stuff to go with it?" he asked.

"Like I said, bro, I ain't got squat," Little Black frowned, "I'm so poor, even the cockroaches done split from my cell."

"We got to have an onion," Berry said, "Tuna just ain't right without onion."

Little Black agreed. Berry flipped the can of tuna in the air, Little Black caught it and said, "We better get busy, and find us an onion."

They looked both ways along the cell row—they were two foxes looking for a turkey. Slow-Talkin' Harry was the only prisoner they saw, but it would be a waste of good breath to ask Harry for an onion. Harry was so tight he squeaked.

They turned their backs on Harry and went off to search the four-story cell block for an onion. Little Black went downstairs and Berry went up.

"Yo, Shorty," Little Black turned into the ground floor cell row and called Shithouse Shorty who was swapping anecdotes and jive with another man. "You got an onion?"

"Naw," Shorty answered, "They make me sweat too much."

"What about some bread?"

"Got two loaves, fresh from the bakeshop. You're welcome to one," Shorty offered, adding, "but payback is a real muthafucker."

"Don't worry about payback," Little Black quipped. "What goes around, comes around."

Shithouse Shorty got the loaf of bread from his cell and handed it to Little Black. Little Black tucked the bread under one arm and went on along the cell row to where Huzzie Bear was mopping the floor.

"Dig it." Little Black slapped Huzzie Bear on the shoulder and caused him to miss a stroke with the mop. "Me and Berry needs an onion," Little Black said. "You got any?"

"Sure do." Huzzie Bear laid the mop aside and asked Little Black for a cigarette.

Black shook three Pall Malls from his pack and joked as he gave them, one at a time, to Huzzie Bear. "One for now, one for later, and one for hard times."

Huzzie Bear said that times were already hard. Little Black knew that to be true, still they were able to laugh as they went to Huzzie Bear's stash in the mop closet under the stairs.

The onions were old and as large as softballs. They had been swagged from the kitchen and were more suited for making soups and stews than for tuna salad sandwiches.

"You got any small, tender ones?" Little Black asked.

"Nope," Huzzie Bear said. "Onion is onion. Whatever you don't use today, you can have tomorrow." He picked three onions from his stash and gave them to Little Black.

"Shee-it!" Little Black jived, "There are enough onions here to make a laughing hyena cry."

Little Black left Huzzie Bear and headed back along the

cell row. The can of tuna was stuffed in his pocket, the loaf of bread was under his arm and the three huge onions were cupped in his hands against his chest.

"Hey, Black," Pee-Wee Brown called as he came into the cell block from the yard, "Let me get some of that bread, man."

"You got any mayo?" Little Black was on point for anything he could get in exchange for some of the bread.

"I ain't got none," Pee-Wee told him, "but Rosewood Willie's got a whole jar. Come on."

Within two minutes Little Black had traded Willie two onions for a cup of mayonnaise with a dab of mustard and a splash of hot sauce stirred in. Willie even threw in the last of a three-day-old pound cake, and Pee-Wee got six slices of bread for arranging the deal.

"What goes around, comes around," Little Black said, and the other two agreed. Black borrowed a paper bag from Willie and dropped in the can of tuna, the remainder of the bread, the pound cake, the cup of mayo and the last of his super onions.

An hour later, by using a combination of begging, bartering, borrowing and con, Little Black's bag was nearly filled when he headed back upstairs to meet Berry.

Berry was waiting at the top of the stairs for Black to come up. Berry wore a satisfied grin on his young face and held a half-full shopping bag in one hand.

"I couldn't find an onion," Berry reported, "but I copped some other stuff." He held the shopping bag open for Little Black to inspect the fruits of his hustling. Berry had managed to parlay two packs of stale cigarettes into three cans of Coke, a dozen leaves of lettuce, six hard-boiled eggs, a package of dehydrated soup, a handful of stuffed olives, two apples, a can of chicken noodle soup, half a Kosher dill pickle, a green bell pepper and a thick slice of medium-rare roast beef. "I couldn't have come off better if I had gone to a supermarket," Berry laughed.

"And this'll be dessert." Little Black reached into his bag and proudly produced the pound cake.

"Man, you ain't say diddly-shit!" Berry was not to be out-done. "Here's the capper. Dig this!" He reached into his bag again and came out with a can of pink salmon.

"Jailhouse caviar," Little Black exclaimed.

"Thanks to me," Berry flipped the can of salmon in his hand, "we're gonna kick back, eat like kings, and chill."

"Don't brag too soon." Little Black handed his bag to Berry. "You start fixing the food, I'll be back in ten." He ran back down the stairs, out the door and across the yard to an-other cell block.

Later, when the guard on duty walked past, making his rounds of the cell block, Little Black and Berry were hunched over plates and bowls of food. They were slurping soup, sip-ping Coke, stuffing down salmon salad sandwiches, nibbling lettuce and eye-balling a dessert of fruit cocktail spread over their pound cake. The inviting combination of fruit and cake was topped with huge gobs of whipped cream.

Although Berry's pink salmon was a real score, Little Black's pound cake with fruit cocktail and whipped cream was even better.

Berry washed down another bite of sandwich. "You still ain't tell me where you got these sweets."

"If I was gonna tell you," Little Black grinned, keeping his secret to himself, "I would have told you already."

"That's good 'n cool with me," Berry's tone was that of a top-billed actor being upstaged by a stand-in. Still he understood that the code of hustlers was much the same as the code of fishermen. When they find a choice spot to make a big catch, neither hustler nor fisherman will give up the location. "As long as we eat regular," Berry conceded, "everything is chill."

After they'd finished eating, Little Black picked up the unopened can of tuna they had started with. It was the only food they had left. "Tomorrow," he said, "we might be able to play this tuna into a chicken dinner."

They both laughed and lit up cigars and puffed like any other businessmen after a profitable day of wheeling and dealing.

◆

The last time we tried a hunger strike the warden stormed into the mess hall and ordered us to eat. When no one made a move to break our solidarity by eating, the warden dragged a large chalkboard into the middle of the mess hall.

"This is your last chance," the warden shouted as he held up a piece of chalk for all to see, then prepared to write. "If you men don't start eating right now," the warden screamed, "I'm going to write the names of every informer, snitch and rat in the prison."

Before the chalk touched the board nearly every plate was clean.

◆

Other than a miserly bit of grey sky, the only thing I can see over the prison wall are the tops of a few trees. I don't know what kinds of trees they are. I don't even care. They are alive and that is all that matters to me.

Year in, year out, we keep each other company. They are

orphaned and outcast also. Their wood is too useless to harvest. They stand in one place and rot. Except for the breath in my lungs, the trees are the most important things in my life.

One tree is friendlier than the others. Its branches spread wide, welcoming arms, inviting birds to rest. Another is not friendly at all. Stark and bare like my cell, it is the Scrooge of the lot—the nemesis of life. Not even leaves stay for long on its branches; even the wind slacks away. A thin tree, a late bloomer, stands alone off to one side, a rejected child still hoping to play. The last of the trees was struck by lightning. Its topmost branch is split like the fork in a country road. This one is my favorite, an extension of myself. In spite of the lightning blows, we survive—mutilated but struggling through the breach nevertheless.

Slow Joe

"Hey, Carlos," Slow Joe called along the row of cells, "How do you spell 'Habeas Corpus'?"

Since Slow Joe was struggling with an appeal of the criminal conviction which brought him to prison, Carlos gladly spelled *Habeas Corpus* for him.

"Hey, Carlos," Slow Joe called again, this time interrupting Carlos' bedtime reading, "How do you spell 'circumstantial evidence'?"

Carlos laid the smut magazine aside, tested his voice to be sure that no traces of being annoyed showed through, then spelled out *Circumstantial Evidence*.

Slow Joe thanked him.

After a while, Carlos tucked himself into bed, turned out his light and went upstairs with a big-breasted woman fantasized from the centerfold of his magazine.

The woman strutted nude, explicit and in living color through the twilight of Carlos' sleep. There was no need for hello's or other time-wasting, getting-to-know-you foreplay. Carlos vented the shutters of his imagination and had just slipped into the woman and bucked twice when Slow Joe called again.

Carlos pushed himself up and reached for the woman. The steel walls and a brace of cell bars greeted his hand.

"Hey, Carlos," Slow Joe shouted, "How do you spell 'victim of circumstances'?"

Carlos shook the sleep from his head, silently cursed Slow Joe for interrupting his dream and answered, "It's spelled M-E."

Slow Joe was quiet for a long time, then he shouted back: "Hey, Carlos, are you sure it's 'M-E'? That don't sound right."

♦

New Year's Eve. A smooth-skinned boy of twenty-one is gang raped in the bathhouse.

The guard on duty puffs an extra-long, mentholated and filtered cigarette and takes his time responding to the screams that are soon gagged away with a bar of prison soap.

When the guard does arrive, the only culprit left to apprehend is the smooth-skinned boy of twenty-one. Blood trickles from the boy's ripped asshole and cum smears his inner thigh like egg white. The stretcher gang arrives and the boy is rushed past the hospital and into a punishment cell.

After the guard checks the correct spelling, he writes his report. The boy is charged with "attempting to incite a riot" with his twenty-one-year-old-smooth-skinned ass.

While the gang rapists boast and plot, the guard lights another cigarette and awaits the next infraction of his bathhouse rules.

♦

Everyone passes the buck. Even when they know the currency is counterfeit and the account is bankrupt, they still pass the buck. No one will stand up or even sit down for anything. The standard offical reply is: "I'll get back to you later." Of course, later keeps getting later, and later, and later and…

Nowhere is the civil service game of CYA—cover your ass—played better than in prison. If anyone asks questions or complains, they can always blame it on the prisoners.

Shit rolls downhill.

Soul Strut

Chaka Kahn shakes her black booty in the warden's wife's face and the guards never understand why we relate to Aretha Franklin when she shouts "Give me R-E-S-P-E-C-T."

Every time the warden sees us snapping our fingers, he smiles and prides himself for keeping us happy. What he doesn't realize is that we snap our fingers to keep our balance when strutting through his bleached out shit.

♦

The day after Easter, the warden posted an order requiring all prisoners to register before practicing the religion of their choice. The decree allows prisoners to attend only those religious services to which the warden approves their fidelity. The new rule does not recognize the realignment of beliefs, nor does it permit spontaneous conversions.

The religious registration forms are the same green color as the alien cards issued to foreigners by the Immigration and Naturalization Service.

Although the new rule may infringe upon the freedom of
religion, the warden views the rule as a blessing. It's an ideal
security arrangement—now he can control prisoners by con-
trolling the exercise of their beliefs.

Some prisoners speculate that for Christmas the warden
will schedule the days of the week when God will be allowed
to visit the prison.

◆

The Warden asks, "How are you?" The guard sergeant
orders, "Cop out," and the shrink drugs those who don't. The
doctor issues an aspirin for everything and signs death certifi-
cates with a grin. The preacher prays with half a lip and hangs
onto his club. The prisoners ease their frustrations by sending
each other to the grave.

Wotowitz

"How would you pronounce this name?"

He printed W O T O W I T Z on a sheet of paper.

"You mean you don't know how to pronounce your own
name?" I looked at the name and tried to figure it out.

"Yeah," he said, "I know my real name, but this is an
alias." He pointed to the name on the paper. "I saw it on a
store sign just before the police busted me. And I've been using it ever since."

"I always wondered where a black dude got such a
name."

"Now you know."

"How would you say it?" I asked him.

He shriveled up his face like a prune. "Wot-o-wits," he
said, "but that don't make it right. I'd be really embarrassed if

someone were to check me on it."

"I know what you mean," I said, still trying to puzzle out the name. "That happened to me once. I was using an alias and the police were about to let me go. Then I opened my fat mouth and mispronounced it. All hell broke loose. I ended up doing two-and-a-half to five and I still never learned to say that name."

◆

Yesterday the homos stopped turning tricks and organized for prison reform. By noon an asshole bandit—as aggressive homo-chasers are called—who was turned down by a prison queen, was knifed by a scared-eyed boy who was protecting his manhood from assault. And two guards were K.O.'d when a pussy hungry weightlifter took their night sticks and went berserk.

The warden, panicked by the sudden violence, agreed on first request to allow TVs in the cells and other reforms if the queens would call off their strike and de-organize. Within an hour the prison was back to "normal" and the warden walked easy.

His only other alternative was to drop his pants and stop the violence himself.

◆

I've been jive, insensitive, and fast-talking. I've left promises unkept and broke every heart that let me in. Now my "help-me" letters come back like stray homing pigeons, stamped "Return to Sender."

◆

Nightwatch

"Yo! You asshole hack," a hard, raking voice shouted down from the dark upper recesses of the blacked-out cell block. "Turn on the heat. I can't do this life sentence like a popsicle!"

Except for the guardroom, and the cell block office, the prison temperature was below freezing. This was the fourth straight night the heat had been turned off. Snow drifted six feet deep in the exercise yard and ice picks of howling wind stabbed in through cracks in the cell block. The wind gusted along the cell rows, looping in and out of the cell bars, going from cell to cell, sucking out what little warmth there was. During the day, when most prisoners were out of their cells for school or work assignments, the cell block was comfortable, almost hot, but at night it was cold.

Prisoners climbed into bed fully dressed. They slept ready rolled in hats, coats, shirts, pants, with extra socks on their hands as mittens, and bathtowels wrapped around their ears. The lucky ones had two blankets. Water froze in the toilets, damp toothbrushes glazed over and coffee left in cups turned to ice.

While the prisoners froze, the nightwatch guard sat comfortably in the warm guardroom. He wore a heavy winter coat when making his rounds of the cell rows, but now the coat was draped over a chair and he was in his shirt sleeves. He had his feet jacked up onto the corner of the desk, a comic book in one hand and a mug of hot chocolate in the other. His portable radio played hillbilly and his fat, red neck dripped sweat.

"Yo, hack!" the voice yelled down from the cold cells, slicing through the hillbilly twang. "Turn on the heat!"

The interruptions annoyed the nightwatch and he

frowned at the sound of the raking voice. He finished his chocolate, put down the comic, slipped into his winter coat and went out into the cold cell block. Breath came from his nostrils like fog. He sneered as he listened to the shouted complaints, raspy voices and choking coughs. Life was an imposition on him, especially the life of a prisoner.

"Knock off the noise," he shouted, hurling threats back at the prisoners. "It's gonna get a lot colder if you keep up the noise."

"The warden's got heat," the hard raking voice yelled again from the top of the darkened cell block. "Why ain't we got none?"

The nightwatch had said everything he had to say, and he wasn't in the mood to argue the point. He started on the ground floor, stomping angrily through the cell block. He ripped from the broken windows the sheets of cardboard the prisoners had placed between themselves and the freezing wind. With the cardboard gone, the wind screamed into the cells like a flight of hawks.

An empty pickle jar, thrown from a dark cell, smashed against the wall and the glass splattered across the cell row ahead of the nightwatch. More bottles and jars were thrown at the nightwatch, but none hit him. He dodged, and then retreated, laughing at the anger he'd provoked. That was his recreation for the night. He cursed them as they had cursed him, then returned to the warm guardroom. He removed his heavy coat, poured another cup of hot chocolate and found his place in the comic book again.

The next day there was no mention of the prisoners' complaints, or even the smashed bottles, in the nightwatch report to the warden. In the morning, when the dayshift guards came on duty, the cell block was warm, and except for a few splinters of glass not swept up by the nightwatch, everything appeared normal. But after the morning head count, when the men were locked out of their cells for the breakfast run to the mess hall, the first guard who opened his mouth to say "Hello" to a prisoner was knocked unconscious and the five other guards who rushed to his aid were beaten senseless.

The riot squad was called. They stormed in and did their work. The prisoners were forced back into their cells, and some had their blood splashed on the concrete floor. The warden claimed not to understand why otherwise well-behaved prisoners would slug a decent guard who greeted them with a cheerful "Hello." Nor did he attempt to find out why. Instead, true to his code, he blamed the prisoners for everything that went wrong. He labeled them "animals" and his myopia precluded any grievances.

That night, the nightwatch left the windows wide open and blasted his radio to drown out any shouts.

Escapes

To remain human in prison,
I had to break the rules.

Checkmate In Cellblock C

FOUR HUNDRED PRISONERS *are locked in steel cells—stacked pigeon holes—one above the other, four tiers high. The prisoners shout from cell to cell. Their voices overlap and generate a cacophony that roars throughout the cell-block like the echo of a wounded beast caged in the bowels of a rail tunnel.*

"Pawn to king-bishop three."

"Stand to your bars! On the count!"

"Screw you, hack!"

"Count your mammy, hack!"

"Who said that?"

"Suck off, pig!"

"Oink! Oink!"

"Bishop to queen-knight two."

"Praise da Lord, 'n keep me near da Cross!"

"Ah, shit! Who woke up the Preacher?"

"Have faith in Him!"

"Preach yo shit, Rev!"

"Pawn to king four."

"There's a mouse in my cell!"

"Dat ain't no mouse. Dat's yo cousin, you rat-bastard!"

"Knock off the noise!"

"Screw you up the butt, pig!"

"Rook to king-rook four."

"That sho' was a dumb move!"

"Shut up and play, sucker!"

"Who's talking about sucking something?"

"Damn! That homo's awake again!"

"Fuck you, Fishmarket! This side of the wall is mine."

"I really wish you fellows would keep the noise down so I
    can rap with my man."

"Shut up, Monique!"

"Pawn to queen-knight three."

"Oya, Juan!"

" 'Oya,' yo mama!"

"Neg-grow, I cut you throat!"

"Queen-side castle."

"I love yooouuu. I love yoouuu. Yes I doooo!"

"Homo, you can't sing!"

"I ain't no homo. I'm Monique, a real-life, living-color
    black woman. That's what I am!"

"Tune out, bitch."

"Your mamma shoulda fed you to the toilet and saved the
    taxpayers the expense of feeding you."

"Knight to queen-bishop five."

"Jo-Jo, I'm'a stick my knife in yo neck!"

"Praise da Lord!"

"Last warning. Knock off the fucking noise!"

"Get lost, hack!"

"You just work here, we live here!"

"Who said that?"

"Your granddaddy's sister said it!"

"Bishop takes knight."

"No matter whatcha say, you is a fag!"

"Suck my pussy! I'm a woman!"

"Goddamit! Which one of you perverts done stole the cen-
    terfold outta my magazine?"

"Slow Joe had it last!"

"Shut up, you snitching cocksucker! You ain't never seen me wid none of them fuckbooks!"

"Pawn takes pawn."

"Nooo-bod-dee knows the trouble I've..."

"Shut up, Do-Dirty! Ain't nobody put that gun in your hand and forced you to do crime!"

"Hey, Pete, what are they serving in the mess hall?"

"Your favorite: Food!"

"Man, leave that fool 'lone. Him's crazy! Every 'hoe he pimped left hair between his teeth!"

"Knight takes pawn."

"Hey, Maxwell! What you do wid all my sugar?"

"He snorted it up his big nose like coke. That's what he did with it!"

"I done told you he be crazy as a shithouse bedbug!"

"Knock off the noise!"

"Fuck you, pig!"

"And your pig-face sister, too!"

"Who said that?"

"My cock said it, hack!"

"Praise da Lord!"

"Preach yo shit, Rev!"

"Pawn to king-knight four."

"Yo, Roundman. I'll see your fat ass in the yard, mudder-fucker!"

"Why wait fo' the yard?"

"Better have your shank ready, 'cause I'm coming out stab-bing!"

"Do-Dirty, I ain't no punk! My record is twenty-and-oh!"

"King to king-bishop two."

"Fishmarket, it don't cost you nothing to stay outta my business!"

"Hey, Monique! If you need a villain in your life, call me.
   Otherwise, leave me alone!"
"Dig it, Jo-Jo! You got any mustard?"
"Whatcha gotta eat?"
"Nothin!"
"Then whatcha want mustard for?"
"Knight to queen-rook three."
"Lord, how'd I ever get into this mess?"
"You got caught, that's how!"
"Knight to queen seven."
"Ain't no place to run!"
"Check!"
"Queen to queen-bishop two."
"They done got the body, and now they want my dreams
   too!"
"Checkmate!"

◆

I envy maggots, crabs and body lice. They have more op-
portunity to make love than I do.

Justice Mike

Justice Mike yanked off the headphones he had plugged
into the prison radio system and threw them to the floor. He
angrily paced his cell, then called out along the cell row to
Sham-God Supreme.
   "I'm gonna write the warden," Justice Mike shouted,
"and get that sex-therapist woman doctor offa our radio."
   "Yeah. Do it. I got your back," Sham-God replied, "I'll
even co-sign the letter. She ain't nothing but a waste of time
when we could be listening to soft-touch music."

"When I first heard she was gonna be on, and talking about sex," Justice Mike yelled from where he sat on the toilet in his cell, "I sure thought she'd be rappin' about real, straight-up, get-down, freaky, funky sex. But all she ever talks about is romance, and I ain't never had no romance. Have you?" Justice Mike asked.

"Not that I can recall," Sham-God Supreme shouted back, "I ain't never even tell nobody that I love them."

◆

I guzzled a batch of jailhouse booze. Then I did two sets of pushups—fifty pushups each set—lifted two hundred pounds of weight ten times and called a fellow prisoner a lively bunch of multi-motherfuckers.

He laughed me off, gave me "peace" and "power" salutes followed by a shout of "Right on, my brother man." Then he strolled away, around the yard, shaking his head as he went. He understood my condition. I was burning off prison tension. Nothing personal. He knew everything in a flash because the day before he had used me in the same way I used him.

"What goes 'round, comes 'round," I thought as I waved the salutes at his back and relaxed against the wall.

Halftrack

Halftrack found her name in a sleazy, third-rate pulp magazine. She was looking for a pen pal, and so was he. Via the U.S. mail, they fell in love and vowed to write every day.

When his long distance lover finally came to visit, she turned out to be a *he* dressed as a *she*.

Now Halftrack vows to blow up the post office.

George

When they let George out of his cell, he walked straight to the middle of the main yard and sat down.

"Fuck it," George said, crossing his legs and making himself comfortable. "Fuck this prison and fuck everything else. The judge sentenced me to do time and this is how I'm going to do it." He spat out a few curse words, then tacked on, "My way."

When the tear gas cleared, George was little more than a pile of flesh dripping blood. Four guards dragged him from the yard and into the mental hospital.

"Fuck it all," George said through the broken teeth, smashed by a guard's club. "If they think I'm crazy now, just wait until I really start doing my time."

Sugar Ditch Pearl

Sugar Ditch Pearl and his lover, Rex, got married in the far corner of the exercise yard, and they spent their honeymoon lifting weights.

Willie

After ten years of jerking off, Willie went home to his wife who had waited with memories of Willie's love. She had stayed in practice, of course, and knew what love making was all about. But Willie, after ten years of non-experience, could only see his wife as a substitute for his fist.

Barracuda and Sheryl

"You can't have this package," the guard in charge of the mailroom told Barracuda. "You'll have to mail it back to the sender." The guard held up a life-size, inflatable rubber doll. The doll was named Sheryl and had the shape of a young woman.

Barracuda had ordered the doll from a hard core porno magazine. The advertisement promised: *"All working parts. Detailed, tight fitting and satisfying. Orifices just like a real woman."* Sheryl was guaranteed to thrill or money back.

"There's no way I can let you have this," the guard said. "Toys are not allowed in this prison, especially not a toy like this doll."

Barracuda persisted, claiming a legal and constitutional right to the doll, to the pursuit of happiness.

"The law is one thing," the guard snapped, "but your perversion is another."

"Perversion?"

"Yes," the guard insisted.

"You got me all wrong." Barracuda made a last ditch effort to get the doll. "I don't want it for myself," he said with a straight face. "I just want to take it out in the main yard and pimp it to other guys."

The guard listened with keen ears for a deal, but when Barracuda failed to make him an offer, the guard confiscated the doll as contraband and ordered Barracuda locked in an observation cell.

The next day, the guard gave Sheryl to Leon Green-Eyes, another pimp, who promised to cut him in on the profits.

Cryin' Shame

Cryin' Shame was the ugliest of the ugly sissies who pranced the prison yard. Razor scars from gut bucket barroom fights lined his pockmarked face like strings on a gypsy's guitar, and when he grinned his snaggle-tooth mouth issued a breath as funky as ten-day-old mustard greens on a hot summer night. Cryin' Shame was so ugly, it was rumored, that when the judge sentenced him to life in prison, he was given an extra year for violating the Environmental Protection Act.

No one ever voluntarily gave Cryin' Shame any action. Not even those asshole bandits who had been in prison and womanless for eons, and were known to fuck anything hot 'n hollow, had the heart to pick Cryin' Shame. Asshole bandits would opt in favor of their fantasies or memories of pre-prison sexual exploits and a greased fist rather than confront the horror of Cryin' Shame's mug.

Over the years, seeded with sexual deprivation, Cryin' Shame had developed a quick, one punch knockout blow. When the mood hit and he longed to be satisfied, Cryin' Shame would engage his prey in pleasant, small talk conversation and coax him off to a quiet, little traveled spot. Then, with his one punch, Cryin' Shame would stun his victim and take what he wanted. As a result, very few unarmed people ever talked to Cryin' Shame. Even the guards kept their distance.

Each time the courts sentenced a new shipment of pig-meat to the prison, Cryin' Shame would be loitering near the reception gate, lurking like a misshapen welcome mat.

One hot summer morning when the yard was in full swing with volleyball and basketball, baseball and handball, chess, checkers and cards, joggers, weightlifters and popcorn pimps polishing their shit, and no one was left inside, Cryin' Shame stalked a new, innocent looking young dude into the storehouse basement.

Before Cryin' Shame could cock his arm and fire his one punch, before he even knew what had hit him, Cryin' Shame's pants had been stripped down around his crusty knees, the cheeks of his bottomless ass had been spread, lightly greased, and the young, innocent looking dude's cum was trickling from Cryin' Shame's butt.

That afternoon, smiling and sashaying like a love-struck school girl, Cryin' Shame displayed the bruises mashed on his chin by the young dude's fist and boasted how he had been raped with tender, loving care.

For days afterward Cryin' Shame hung out in the storehouse basement. He waited like a mark to be mugged. After a week had passed and nothing happened—not even an accidental bump followed by an apologetic "Excuse me"—Cryin' Shame shuffled around the exercise yard and lamented that a one-punch love affair is worse than no love affair at all.

♦

"I don't know why I'm writing to you," a thirteen-year-old girl wrote, "except I want to find out. But don't want to sound nosey. Because I'm not.

"I don't even care if you really did what the newspapers say you did, or even if you are an evil person and should be locked away in prison.

"I was lonely once. Not like you must be. But I was sick in the hospital, and no friends came to see me.

"So I know a little about how you must feel.

"Are you also afraid to die?"

Ronnie Too-Sweet

"Hit a woman?" Ronnie Too-Sweet said. "Man, you have got to be crazy or smokin' dope. I once beat my girlfriend and she ran off and joined the Marines. When she came home, she told me they had treated her worse than I ever did. But don't you know, in the meantime she had learned to fight."

Hank

Hank pulled his hat down over his ears and tucked a bath towel around his neck and into the collar of his heavy, oversized, winter coat. He stamped his boots in the snow and paid little attention to the four younger men gathered around a table in the yard. The four drank hot coffee and pontificated how they were going to serve out the long prison sentences they faced.

Hank had heard it all before, many times over. There was nothing new the young men could say. Each new crop of prisoners brought new variations of an old theme. Their conversation was a remake of an old movie.

After each young man had said his piece, he turned to Hank for his advice.

"Ain't much advice I can give," Hank said thoughtfully. "You came to prison on your own, so you'll each have to do the time on your own. You can drink jailhouse wine, and talk bull, or you can turn yourself over to the shrink and space out on his drugs. This prison ain't gonna offer other alternatives. So," Hank looked each of the young men in the eyes, "your best bet is to drink wine and bullshit. That's the lesser of two evils."

♦

Exams are designed for the poor. Rich folks don't take exams. They make them up to keep us confused. They hand out an exam and say, "If you pass this we'll let you move up into the 'clique'." But most of the questions don't have any answers. Like asking, "How many hairs are on a square inch of a sheep's skin?"

Hell, the only time I ever saw a sheep's skin was when it was on something I stole.

Shing-a-Ling and China

At one time in the joint, there was Shing-a-Ling.

As prison slick kids go, Shing-a-Ling was a minor leaguer, but you could never tell him that. We both worked in the prison's maintenance shop. He was in charge of tools; he'd issue them, receive them, clean and put them away. I handled the inventories, the typing and the filing. There was never much work and plenty of time to talk.

One summer day, while working and listening to Sam Cooke sing *"You Send Me"* over the shop's radio, Shing-a-Ling said to me: "Man, I'm in love. In love like a mudderfucker."

"Beautiful," I said as I went on with my work. "Solid on that. Who's the lucky broad?"

"The new queen."

"The new what?" I put my work aside and looked at him.

"The new queen. Name is China 'cause of that mellow, high yellow shine, and them slanted eyes."

"Wait one minute," I said. "Give me a replay. Slow-drag that past me again."

"She digs me."

"She? That's a man." I emphasized the words: "A man. Spelled M-A-N. Man."

"I know." He lit a cigarette and blew a cloud of smoke. "But the dude is fine. Super fine."

"You crazy?"

"No jive."

"Shit."

"No bull. I'm serious."

He pushed himself up from the chair and bopped around the room. "I laid my heaviest game down, and China went for it. Fact is, she ain't have no choice 'cept to go for it. Couldn't resist." He laughed and slapped his thighs. "Man, when Shing-a-Ling plays the tune, everybody dances."

"You better cool your role." I sipped my coffee and went back to filing the morning maintenance reports. "Next," I said, "you'll be strutting and swishing and carrying on around here like a go-go dancer."

"I'm a thoroughbred player." He poured himself a cup of my coffee, mixed in cream and sugar, took a sip and said, "I'm a pimp, not a simp. I can con a swan. My game is playing game, not being lame."

"Don't pad your part," I cautioned him, "If you deal, you'll shuffle; if you pitch, you'll catch. So, dig yourself."

Another routine week of prison life passed. The matter was out of mind until Shing-a-Ling said, "Dig it. I got that broad uptight. The chick really digs me."

"Who?" I was busy typing the monthly inventory.

"China. My queen. Remember?"

I continued to hunt 'n peck on the typewriter and asked, "What makes you figure 'it' digs you?"

"Keep this under your hat, Jay." He grinned and his face radiated pride. "Read this bulletin the broad laid on me."

Shing-a-Ling handed me the note which I unfolded with caution. It was a plainly printed message and I almost died choking back my laughter.

"Hey good buddy," I smiled up at him. "Are you sure this is the right note?"

"Damn is."

"Then what makes you think that your game is on target?"

"Says so right there." He pointed to the note in my hand. "Says she loves me."

"Man," I asked as discreetly as possible, "can you read?"

The smile drained from his face.

"What do it say?" His voice was a whisper.

"Here." I held the note out to him. "Read it again."

Shing-a-Ling hesitated. "Jay," he said, "I can't read."

"Man, spare me the dumb shit."

"Really, I can't."

"Don't pull that I-can't-read game on me," I laughed.

He stood fallen-shouldered and looking at the floor.

"Jay," his voice was humble, "not more than three people in this here joint know the truth, but man, I really can't read."

The humor was gone.

I looked up at him, and looked at the note, and remembered the many times I had watched Shing-a-Ling lug his tome of sports facts and records through the Control Gate and into the maintenance shop—coming like Moses down the mountain to settle an angry argument. How many times had I laughed as he defiantly hurled the volumes down and spat out the challenge: "There, you jive turkey. Read page 634. Read and weep." He'd shout, "Read out loud, so everybody can hear how dumb you really are."

And too, how many times had I played the sucker and

lunged for the greasy pig by going for his letter-from-home game—always starting with him moping around in a blue mood and ending with me being hustled into reading his mail aloud.

And in the main yard, when dealing with the smut merchants, Shing-a-Ling would say, "Dig it. I read slow, so just mark off the pages where the action is heavy; where they is gettin' down to the real funky stuff. Mark the pages and I'll take it from there." Then later that evening in the cell block after we were all locked in and settled for the night, Shing-a-Ling would break the quiet with loud guffaws and bumps against his neighbors' wall until one of them would holler over to him, "Hey man, what the fuck is with you?" And Shing-a-Ling would reply, "Homeboy, this book is a mudder-fucker. These people is gettin' down to some real freaky mess." That was the lure. As soon as the guy would say, "Turn me on to it," Shing-a-Ling would say, "All right. Here." He'd pass the book through the bars and over to the next cell. "Read those pages where it's marked," Shing-a-Ling would say. "Read it out loud. Read it so that I can hear, too."

And that's the way it always went.

Now he was standing in front of me saying, "Please read the note. Jay, what do China say?"

I was embarrassed for him. Still, he insisted I read the note.

"*You jive-time sonofabitch,*" I read China's message aloud. "*You ain't man enough for me. Furthermore that thing between your legs ain't nothing but a handle for me to turn you over with. So, if you ever try your popcorn-pimp shit with me, you will soon find out who the real whore is.*" The note was signed "China," with a postscript: "*Don't fuck with anything you can't handle.*"

When I had finished reading, Shing-a-Ling was devastated. He said nothing. He just took the note from my hand

and folded it into his shirt pocket and walked from the shop.

He didn't return to work that day. And when he didn't show up the next morning, I went looking for him. On my way across the yard I ran into Nifty Green, one of Shing-a-Ling's slick sidekicks.

"You seen Shing-a-Ling?" I asked.

"Him's a changed dude," Nifty said, flicking his hands, making sure I saw his newly manicured fingernails. "Him's done changed overnight."

"What's he done?"

"Him's done gone over to the other side. Done squared-up on me and the fellows." Nifty frowned as if the words left a nasty taste on his tongue. "Him's acting like a pedigree, middle-class square."

"Where is he?"

"In the school." Nifty frowned again.

I left Nifty in the middle of the yard, still flashing his fingernails and looking pseudo-slick.

When I got to the school the class period had just ended and the halls were jammed with men, but I didn't see Shing-a-Ling anyplace.

"You seen Shing-a-Ling?" I asked Cleanhead, the inmate clerk in the school's office.

"Yeah," Cleanhead said, looking up from his work, "Shing-a-Ling is in the Learning Lab."

I turned the corner and stepped into the room.

Shing-a-Ling was sitting at the study table, his head bent forward into the learning booths. He was wearing earphones and didn't hear me walk over. For a few seconds I stood behind him reading over his shoulder and watching him flip the pages of the book and mouth the words he heard through the earphones.

"SEE DICK RUN. SEE JANE RUN. SEE DICK AND JANE RUN."

He sensed my presence, shut off the tape player, removed the earphones and looked up as he turned to me.

"Hey now, Jay," he said. "What is it?"

"You tell me."

"Gettin' this reading thing together." He smiled.

"That's hip," I said.

"That homo done checked my game. Turned me 'round. Did a number on me." His voice was glum, but he managed to keep a smile. "But all that's cool. I done learned a big lesson," he told me. "If a player ain't got an end game, he ain't got no game at all."

"True."

"But you can't play the game at all, 'less you can read the bulletins when they come."

"I can dig it."

"So," he said, "I'm gettin' it together."

"Solid," I said and started to leave.

"One favor?" he asked.

"Name it."

"Don't call me Shing-a-Ling any more."

I was blank.

"Call me my real name. It's nicer."

"Sure," I said, "What is it?"

"Vernon Alonzo Bowen. It sounds square, but it's me."

I smiled for him.

He said, "Excuse my back," and put on the earphones again. He turned on the tape player and went back to reading and mouthing the words as he listened. "SEE DICK RUN. SEE JANE RUN. SEE DICK AND JANE RUN."

Lizard MacDonald

The only time Lizard MacDonald laughs is when he's busy joking and clowning for the guards. His stylized Step'n Fetchit is more of an insult than all the myths about Uncle Tom.

He doesn't scratch his nappy head or shuffle his slew feet. Those old fashioned stereotypical routines of servile comedy aren't for him. Lizard MacDonald is contemporary; he's up to date, a polished practitioner of progressive slavery who grins "Right on!" instead of "Yessum, Boss."

He often oversports his role, playing his part well beyond the hilt. Prisoners avoid him and his ass-kissing embarrasses the guards. The chaplain views him with suspicion; to him Lizard has other motives, a hidden agenda not even the prison shrink can figure out. The warden claims to be unconcerned, still he wonders why Lizard works so hard to please while other prisoners are plotting to riot.

◆

Room Number 1—called The Space Station—is the prison hospital's psycho observation room. There is nothing in this room except a mattress on the floor, a bare bulb in the ceiling and ghosts of minds out of control.

Every night, shrieks and howls from Room Number 1 sound across the empty yard. They remind us, caged in the cells, that going over the wall is not the only escape.

As in a game of chance where every number is a potential winner, in prison every inmate is a potential space case. We all have an inside story waiting to be screamed across the yard.

◆

The next morning they told us that the screams had come from a prisoner who couldn't cope and had gone berserk in his cell. They went on to explain that the blood splattered on the basement wall had come when the prisoner had slipped headlong down the stairs, and had cut his lip, smashed his nose, and broke his jaw against the boot of the guard sergeant who had tried to help him up. We nodded, and thanked them for the information and their time. That night we slept with earplugs.

Eddie E.

Now take Eddie E.. He's been through prison lockdowns, riots, hunger strikes, gallons of jailhouse booze, threats from racist guards, a number of indifferent wardens and a bevy of psychiatrists, too.

No one has ever had to put into words the meaning of courage and dignity for his life. Eddie E. would glean the stalks of another's harvest and go without before he'd beg. He never shuffles. He never bows. Each step is high and proud.

"He's arrogant," say the guards.

"He's an example," say the prisoners.

Eddie E. says nothing. He just holds his head up and refuses to let his shoulders slouch.

◆

"I wonder what the world is doing out there," I mused as I stared at the top of the lone tree that showed over the prison wall.

"Whatever the world is doing," Peewee, a streetwise realist, reminded me, "the world is doing it without us."

Frankie Cool, who'd just received a Dear John from his woman, said, "You've sure got that right."

The three of us went to sit under the guntower to forget about trees, the world and the authors of letters that begin with: "I will always love you, but I thought you ought to know..."

♦

Carl's wife sent him a Dear John. He threw the letter into the toilet and the toilet threw it back.

Revolutionary Frankie

When Frankie came to prison he chanted revolutionary slogans and changed his name to a Mau-Mau sobriquet that sounded like a threat to the warden.

Frankie's aggressive attitude intimidated guards and made fellow prisoners aware of their bondage. A few prisoners, following Frankie's example, took a stand against the system. But most yelled curses only when the lights were out and their faces couldn't be seen.

Frankie strutted his liberation rhetoric and condemned any who didn't share his zeal. However, in the dark, when his revolutionary fervor dozed and his strident self-image hung like a an oversized raglan coat on the bars of his cell, Frankie could find no way to rationalize the rape-murder of the sixty-nine-year-old grandmother with arthritic hands and swollen, tree-trunk ankles. Nor could he explain away any of the other sex crimes that sent him to prison.

Alone, at night, Frankie feasted on self-hate.

Crazy Willie

Crazy Willie talked to fairies and counted blades of grass. He spent time with Moses, Dante, Mohammed and Buddha. Even the presidents of the United States were numbered among his daily friends.

When Willie went to church, he spoke with God. The chaplain thought that was worthy, if not spiritually cool. But when Willie insisted that God had spoken to him, the chaplain reported him to the guard sergeant. The sergeant charged Willie with "unauthorized communications" and turned him over to the shrink. The shrink fitted Willie with a tight white jacket, filled his veins with chemical peace and booked him into a padded cell.

When Willie came back from the mental hospital we still called him Crazy Willie. But Willie wasn't so crazy as not to know that he could talk with anyone, except himself, and even then, never out loud.

Old Vinnie

"This place ain't no prison any more," Old Vinnie shouted his weekly tirade into the face of a young, new-jack guard, and then ambled out of the cell block for the afternoon sun. "This place is a mental institution," Vinnie shouted again, and the guard backed a few steps away. "This might look like a prison, but it's really a damn bughouse."

The young guard looked around for assistance, but none of the other guards patrolling the yard bothered to look his way. They each had had their day with Old Vinnie, now it was the new-jack's turn. The other guards focused their attention elsewhere and left the new-jack to stand alone.

"Young guys coming to prison nowadays," Vinnie shouted, "they need to be in a bug ward, not in a cell. The standards have been lowered all around. It's a damned disgrace. Now anybody who don't know any better can come to prison: it's as easy as going to eat in one of those fast-food joints. Ain't no quality in prison no more." He took a few steps away from the young guard, then he turned back to serve the rest of his sermon. "And that includes these bums you work with. They call themselves 'Corrections Officers.' Crap!" Vinnie spat out the words. "It would take two dozen of these creeps to make one good old-time hack. And you, sonny—" Vinnie wiggled a finger in the new-jack's face "—you'll never measure up. Even the warden is a mental case."

Vinnie let out a sad sigh as if commiserating with himself. Then he turned away from the guard and went across the yard to sit in the sun.

The other guards avoided the young guard for the rest of that day. No one wanted to look him in the eyes. No one was ready to admit to him that old Vinnie was right.

◆

I used to have a large, nude pin-up on my cell wall. It was there, across from the bed, doing time just as I was, until I woke up from a wet dream and in the half light thought a naked woman was in the cell with me.

When fantasies become that real, it's time to give them up.

The next time I pin up a photograph, it will be of something I can use—like a helicopter.

Rock Candy

"So I told the whore, 'Love me or leave me,' " Rock Candy explained as he rocked on the balls of his feet. "Now she's been gone six months and the only word I got was a 'Get Well' card on Christmas Day."

Latamore

Everybody called Latamore a bug, a space case, or just plain crazy. No one took him seriously. Especially when he told about the nuclear submarine that he was building in his cell and how he would flush himself down the john and escape to cruise the South China Sea with Peter Lorre and Doctor Fu Manchu. Or about the helicopter that was nearly complete and would lift him over the wall and into a harem of mink-cunted nymphs.

He was on everyone's pay-him-no-mind list. Still, Latamore was as happy as a madam counting the take and often said, by way of a caveat, that he would escape and we would be left behind—asleep.

On the morning of the day that they cut Latamore down from the bars and painted over the marks from his rubber heels where, like a salmon going upstream, he had kicked himself to freedom, the guard sergeant asked us if we had heard anything during the night. The best that we could do was to lower our eyes and testify that when Latamore had made good his solo escape to the South China Sea and a world of mink-cunted nymphs, the rest of us were having nightmares.

No one had the heart to mention that we all had separate escape plans of our own.

Huzzie Bear

"That's out-and-out, unadulterated, high-grade, sexist bullshit!" Huzzie Bear loudly denounced Sham-God Supreme's assertion that all liberated women are frustrated men-haters suffering from penis envy. "Machismo is dictatorship in the bedroom," Huzzie Bear declared.

Everybody in the chowline, including Clutch Cargo and another female guard who had escorted the prisoners to the mess hall, turned and looked in Huzzie Bear's direction.

"You've got a real screwed-up head problem," Huzzie Bear fumed at Sham-God. Huzzie stomped one foot and then the other, like a sumo wrestler warming up for a match. "Just because you hate all women, don't mean that all women hate men."

"The bitches are taking over." Sham-God tried to defend his indefensible position. He looked around for support from others in the chowline, but no one gave it to him.

"Pro-female doesn't mean anti-male," Huzzie Bear pointed out.

"Just look what they've done to Wall Street, the Army, Navy and Marines," Sham-God said.

"Unless women have full equal rights," Huzzie Bear asserted, "and can decide when, where and with whom, we men will continue to practice colonialism when we should be making love."

"And now," Sham-God went on, "we got broads driving big-rig trucks, and some who want to play football, too. If that ain't proof, then what is?"

Enough had been said; now Huzzie Bear was ready to end the conversation by cramming an angry fist into Sham-God's mouth.

Sham-God took one look at Huzzie Bear's balled fist and

bit back his words. He wanted to change the subject, but Huzzie Bear refused to give him anymore rap.

"If you keep running off at the mouth," Huzzie Bear warned him, "I'm going to shut you up."

Sham-God clamped his lips tightly together and adjusted his eyeglasses higher onto his wide nose. He was quiet now and thinking about the twenty-five years he was serving for rape.

◆

When the chief psychiatrist fired his inmate clerk the guard sergeant asked, "Why?"

"He's a model prisoner, the kind the system is proud to produce," the shrink described the clerk to the sergeant, then went on to explain, "but he has been on the job for two full years and two years is long enough for any person to work any one job."

The sergeant raised an eyebrow but wisely kept his mouth shut. The psychiatrist, like J. Edgar Hoover, knows something about everybody. Not even the warden will speak against him.

After the prisoner was recycled and readjusted from clerk with responsibility to a clean-up man with mop and broom, the sergeant asked the psychiatrist, jokingly, of course, if the shrink planned to change jobs also. "Maybe," the sergeant chuckled, "you will reassign yourself from the head of the 'Space Station' to a mess hall cook."

Of course, in public, the psych laughed it off, but in private he made a note in the guard sergeant's file.

Now every time a new batch of replacements arrive from the training academy, the sergeant looks over his shoulder, and like the mark in a loaded crap game, he waits for the axe to fall.

Ronny Red

Ronny Red served thirteen straight years and every day was hard time in maximum security. He had one fight. The other man went to the hospital with a broken jaw and Ronny was locked in an isolation cell for six months. Except for that one fight, Ronny was super cool. He obeyed all rules, was never in the wrong place, and followed every order no matter how dumb the guard who gave it. He worked scrubbing floors for fifty-five cents a day and answered "Yes sir" or "No sir" even when it wasn't required.

Ronny Red did everything possible to be right. He broke old habits and saved half his pay each week. His savings would help him start a new life when he got out of prison. The rest of his money went to support his basic needs; he bought soap and toothpaste and treated himself to an ice cream at the commissary every other week.

When Ronny went before the three parole commissioners in the hope of gaining his release, the only black mark on his record was the fight he'd had many years before. The parole commissioners overlooked the fight, and overlooked everything good he'd done as well. Instead they dragged out a judge's bench warrant, more than fifteen years old, and charged Ronny with delinquent child support payments.

The judge who signed the warrant was long dead from a heart attack, but his signature was still legal. The commissioners appropriated Ronny's savings account and ordered him held in prison until he paid in full.

Ronny Red had never seen the son the judge's warrant claimed he fathered. He couldn't remember the mother's name, or the bar where they met. The only memory he had when he left the parole hearing was of the cigarette butts the commissioners had crushed on the floor—a floor he'd have to scrub clean.

Jim-Bo

"I wanta tell you…" Jim-Bo hitched up his baggy prison-issued pants and interrupted a group of men who were talking at the side of the handball court. "When something good comes," Jim-Bo said, "it's gonna come on a Monday."

A couple of men took offense at Jim-Bo for breaking into their conversation and shot him hard, cold stares. But the ones who knew Jim-Bo ignored him and went on talking as if he didn't exist.

"You know what I mean?" Jim-Bo's words became a backdrop to the conversation around him. "Something really good, like people mobbing together to end all this crazy shit that politicians been laying on us common folk. Stuff like unemployment and hunger and all this nuke-atomic crap. Poisoning folks with chemicals, polluting the air, land and sea, and making cars and airplanes and jive-time can openers that don't work right."

Jim-Bo's thick grey hair was as wild as a pack of wolves on night patrol. He walked bent forward with one shoulder lower than the other and carried his head at an awkward angle. Twenty-eight years behind the prison wall had sapped the luster from his pecan-brown skin and sucked the light from his eyes. The prison dentist had taken all of his teeth and he had accidentally flushed the plastic replacement down the toilet. The psych certified him "borderline but harmless," and most everybody else had him on their pay-him-no-mind list.

"No, sir," Jim-Bo went on, unconcerned that no one listened to him. "It won't be a Wednesday when something good comes. Wednesdays are good days already, and nothing can make them any better. They're cool-out days, lay-back days—they smooth out the hump in the middle of the week." He said, "We just sort of cruise through our Wednesdays, so can't nothing gooder than that ever happen on a Wednesday.

"And Fridays, well…" He scratched the side of his head and appeared somewhat depressed. "Nothing good is gonna happen on a Friday," he said without enthusiasm. "It's the end of the week and people want to rush home for the weekend. So even if something good was to come to us, nobody would pay it any attention." He thought for a moment and added, "And there's always the big risk of running into a Friday the Thirteenth!"

The other men turned their backs and raised their voices to drown out Jim-Bo.

"Tuesdays and Thursdays are out of the question," Jim-Bo ranted on, unperturbed by the indifference the other men showed him. "There's nothing good to say about Tuesdays and Thursdays. They just sort of hold the rest of the week together." He stopped talking long enough to collect his thoughts and figure out what to say next. "And weekends are party days," he continued with a tinge of excitement as if remembering his good times. "On weekends ain't nobody got any time for revolution. So, if something real good is gonna come to us, it's gonna happen on a Monday." He was amused with himself and rocked back and forth on the balls of his feet. "There's no better way to start a fucked-up week than to have something good come your way."

One by one the other men wandered off, leaving Jim-Bo alone at the side of the handball court. The handball game came to an end and even the players went off to do other things.

Jim-Bo was not bothered by the departure of his audience, nor was he daunted. He walked up to the first guard he saw and picked up talking to finish what he'd started telling the men at the handball court.

"It's just gotta be a Monday," Jim-Bo spoke to the confused guard. "I'm planning on it, and I don't want to change my plans again."

The guard stepped around Jim-Bo and continued to patrol the yard. Jim-Bo was left with his mouth hung open. He had his words ready to speak, but no one to speak them to.

"That's right," he muttered to himself as he looked down at his shoes. "It's bad enough being in prison without having to change my plans all the time."

The next morning—Tuesday—the day-shift guard found Jim-Bo dead. One end of his belt was looped around his neck, the other end was knotted around the coathook high up on the steel wall of his cell.

Willie Neckbone, Wizard & Noonie

Willie Neckbone and his partner Wizard staggered past. I gave them a friendly wave from my seat where two cell blocks joined to form a corner at one end of the exercise yard.

The wine had hit them hard. Willie leaned heavily on Wizard for support, and Wizard supported himself with a hand against the cell block wall. They struggled for balance and then took a few more drunken steps. They seemed unsure of their legs, and I doubted they could make it the rest of the way around the yard.

Wizard pushed away from the wall, and the two of them almost went down, but they managed to steady themselves and maneuver onto the Iron Pile, a collection of mismatched weights where body builders and heavy lifters worked out. There they rested.

Willie was lanky, with big, melancholy brown eyes and a long neck. The bones stood out on the back of his neck, and when he talked his lumpy Adam's Apple slid up and down the length of his skinny throat. His lower lip was thick and his jaw was as square as a boxcar. His hair needed combing, and he had forgotten to zip his fly.

Wizard was a head shorter than Willie with more meat on his bones, but far less hair on his head. His skin had a dusty pallor, like parched earth, and his prison-issued teeth rattled when he talked and slipped loose from his gums when he opened his mouth to laugh.

Willie bragged that he'd been a fast-working con man who had played every con game known. "And," as he put it, "I even invented a few games of my own." When he was so-ber—which he seldom was—he could fast-talk double-talk; his rap was as smooth as a golfer's stroke. Sober, Willie could sell condoms to a eunuch. But when wine tied his tongue, he stammered and left words out of his sentences. He'd forget what he was saying and even who he was saying it to. But he was always good for a laugh and never got offended, even when the joke was on him.

I watched Willie and Wizard stagger away from the Iron Pile and head toward the handball courts. They were an awk-ward duo, yet they were a perfect match. Willie supplied the humor and Wizard supplied their daily drink: two quarts of jailhouse wine.

Wizard had a long history of short terms in local jails and was now serving his second sentence in maximum secu-rity for auto theft. He'd never had much success as an outlaw, but he could make wine from almost anything.

When he couldn't swag fruit and juice from the kitchen, Wizard made wine from canned fruit cocktail, adding Kool-Aid for color, and a raw potato to ferment the brew. It was said that he could make a batch of wine from Campbell's Chicken Noodle Soup, sugar, and a few hunks of mess hall bread. Although it was unlikely that this could be done, Wizard's rep as a winemaker was tight enough to sustain the belief.

Willie and Wizard steadied themselves at the side of a table, then started across the open yard. Midway, Willie caught his toe on a clump of grass, tripped and went down, hard. He managed to come up to one knee, but he couldn't coordinate the effort to stand up. Wizard bent, offering a helping hand to his pal, but instead of pulling Willie up from the ground, Wizard was pulled down on top of Willie. First they blamed each other for the mishap. Then they did what they spent most of their time doing—helping each other up.

Even though Willie Neckbone and Wizard did a great job of staying drunk, they still came across as third-rate character actors trying to impersonate real winos.

"Now take good old Noonie," I thought, remembering John Henry Efrain "Noonie" Reese from my boyhood days. In contrast to Willie and Wizard, Noonie was a thoroughbred among winos. He had integrity.

Noonie's head was too large for his squat body. "Water on the brain at birth," the old folks in the neighborhood alleged. His ears lay flat against his head and his nose, broken in a street fight, sat slightly off-center on his moon face. Even when he wasn't drunk—a rare community event worth celebrating—Noonie still staggered when he walked.

He was the son of the neighborhood plumber and the nephew of our fourth grade teacher, both respected deacons in the Baptist church. Among the older people, Noonie was more tolerated than liked, but it was different with us twelve and thirteen year-old boys. He was our avenger, our outlaw warrior. Noonie was everything our mothers begged Jesus to deliver us from.

At the time, Noonie was the only person in our neighborhood other than Reverend Martin who had served in the military. However, for Noonie it had been a short stay. His military career ended almost before it started; still, or so he said, it was long enough for him to have had daring exploits and wild escapades in every corner of the world. Old people always expressed their doubts with raised eyebrows or a dismissive, "Right. Sure thing," but we boys never challenged him, or tried to prove him a liar. We all knew that it was as natural for Noonie to mix fact with fiction as it was for him to drink, so for us the truth of his life didn't matter. Listening to his "war stories" was an adventure and that was good enough for us.

Every Saturday evening during the summer, some of us boys would meet under the streetlight at the corner of the playground. We were old enough to be out of the house for an hour after dark but too young to tag along with the older boys, and much too young to even think about taking a girl and a blanket into the woods by the lake.

The playground was a lumpy, rutted field where weeds and crabgrass had been cut short enough to play softball and to pitch horseshoes. There wasn't any sidewalk, just a widening of the hard-packed red dirt at the side of the street. The streetlight at the corner was the only one left working for blocks around. This was our Saturday evening meeting place, so we hadn't used it as a target for our slingshots.

We'd start gathering at the corner around dusk. There'd be five or six of us by the time the streetlight came on, and two or three more would join us soon afterwards. Noonie would show a little later. It was as if he'd been watching and waiting until everyone who was coming had come before making his appearance. We'd see him staggering toward us, right down the middle of the street. If a car came along, the driver would have to swerve around him. In our neighborhood, old folks, small children, dogs and Noonie had the right-of-way.

He'd come shuffling along, never really lifting his feet from the ground. It was as though he was afraid he wouldn't remember how to put them down again if he picked them up. Noonie's shuffling stagger was a distinguishing characteristic, a trademark by which I later came to measure all other winos.

Without fail, Noonie always broke the ice of his arrival with a few jokes. And after we all had a good laugh, he'd suggest we have a drink. "Nothing big," Noonie invariably said, "Just a nip to round the rough edges offa life and lift our spirits a bit."

Since Noonie was always broke—his pockets on E for empty—and he was forever waiting to be paid for a job we all knew he never worked, we boys always chipped in our nickels, dimes, and an occasional quarter to buy a quart of Gallo white port wine and a small bottle of lemon juice. Sometimes we'd have enough for a quart of tap beer and a dozen large, twisted pretzels. Usually the pretzels were stale, but they'd still taste good, and the beer, mostly foam with the flavor of an oaken keg, came in a tall, waxed white cardboard container.

We'd count out our money, double-checking to the last cent before entrusting it to Noonie. Sometimes three, but never fewer than two of us went along with him to Sam's Liquor Store on the highway, about a half mile away.

The highway divided our neighborhood from the white neighborhood. A few white families lived on our side of the highway, but there weren't any black families on their side. Our white families had lived with us for generations. They went to church and school with us, played on our teams, came to our picnics and were buried in our graveyard. Skin color wasn't a criterion for judging each other's character. It was only when we crossed the highway into the all-white neighborhood that color became a problem. Consequently, few black people ever bothered to cross the highway, except when going to and from work, and about the only time any of us boys even went near the highway was when we'd escort Noonie to buy our Saturday evening wine.

While Noonie went into Sam's store, one of us waited out front and another watched the alley behind the store. Although we honored Noonie as our free-wheeling hero, we knew from bitter experience that he wasn't to be trusted unwatched with our wine. We'd learned that lesson over and again. More than once Noonie had disappeared with the wine, leaving us to wait for him under the streetlight—kicking our Buster Browns at the hard, red dirt and cursing the loss of our nickels and dimes.

Two or three days later, Noonie would show up. He'd act as if he was suffering from amnesia, confessing no recollection that he was supposed to return from Sam's with a bottle of wine. If Noonie could have gotten away with it, he'd deny knowing us at all. We got burned and learned. Still we loved him. After all, there was no one else in our neighborhood—and therefore in the whole world—like him. Everybody else worked hard, was law abiding and feared God. Drinking was Noonie's religion and the only thing he feared was not having enough wine to drink.

When Noonie and the boys chaperoning him returned under the streetlight, he'd be carrying the bottle wrapped in a brown paper bag. First he'd offer a toast, which was his way of saluting the wine. This was a solemn occasion, a ritual. He'd lower the tone of his voice and chant his words with the rhythm of a heartbeat. He'd weave his words into a ballad-like poem that told a story about history's great drinkers from Bacchus to Stagger-Lee. Throughout, Noonie would sprinkle his narrative with what he claimed were Greek, Latin and African words that originally came from the lips of ancient wine drinkers. According to Noonie, he was the lineage holder of a secret society, and these words had been passed down and entrusted to him in the same way that The Word was entrusted to Reverend Martin.

After the toast, he'd command, "Mark the spot," and one of us boys would use a stick to scratch a large circle in the ground, and then a smaller circle inside the larger one. Noonie, with the wine bottle still tightly wrapped in the paper bag, would step to the center of the inner circle and we boys would spread ourselves around the larger outside circle.

Noonie would hold the bottle around the neck with one hand and give the bottom of the bottle a sharp whack with the heel of his other hand. "Waking up the wine. Giving it life," Noonie said, "the same as when a doctor slaps the bottom of a newborn child." Then with the flair of a carnival showman, he'd break the seal, screw off the bottle cap and lick the inside of the cap, carefully tonguing out the droplets of wine. "Got to enjoy everything in this life," he said, " 'cause we don't know a thing about the next life." Raising the bottle high above his big head, he'd offered another toast, a prayer of thanksgiving. This toast, he alleged, purified the wine and made it drinkable by removing the "grimies" that could make us puke and cause hangovers.

Next, he poured a few drops of wine on the ground, inside the small circle. This was our sacrifice, which according to Noonie, hallowed the ground on which we stood and witnessed our kinship with Mother Earth.

As a final offering, he spilled another few drops outside the small circle but inside the larger one. "This is for the brothers upstate," he said. We never questioned who the "brothers" were, nor where they were "upstate," but after the judge sentenced me I learned that "upstate" referred to prison and the "brothers" were prisoners.

Once the toasts and sacrifices were made, Noonie joined us boys in the line around the larger outside circle. He was always the first to drink. "I'm taking off the poison," he announced as he raised the bottle, still wrapped in the paper bag, to his lips. If we didn't watch Noonie carefully, he'd drop his head back as far as it would go on his neck, close his eyes and turn the bottle straight up in line with his throat and chug-a-lug huge, gluttonous gulps of wine. He sounded like a drainage sewer sucking down backed-up rain water. Air would bubble up through the white wine, and we'd have to move quickly to keep him from drinking the bottle dry. We'd remind him that we wanted to drink, too. Without fail, he'd look innocent, as if he'd done no wrong and was being unjustly accused of a major crime. In defense, he'd push the paper bag down from around the neck of the bottle and hold it up to the streetlight so we could all see the level of the wine. "I wasn't trying to beat you for your share," he'd say, making sure that his was the tone of a victim. "I was only making room to pour in the lemon juice." We could never bring ourselves to call him a liar. He'd look sad and hurt, and his expression never failed to make us feel ashamed for not trusting him. Invariably, to make amends, one of us would say, "Take another little sip for yourself, Noonie. We ain't mad at you." This "little sip" was our peace offering, which Noonie always tried to stretch into a long swig. This would lead to another round of accusations from us and denials from him. We couldn't embarrass him and he was insult-proof. In that way, he was beautiful. He had a ready excuse for everything, and we'd heard them all. Still, no matter what he did, we went along with him. After all, Noonie was our hero, an intrepid wino and a community treasure.

One of us boys would open the bottle of lemon juice and Noonie would carefully pour some of it into the bottle of wine. He'd take a sip, testing the mixture to be sure it was the correct blend, and then our drinking would start.

While the bottle passed from boy to boy, going around the circle, Noonie told jokes and recounted his misadventures in the Army. His speaking cadence was punctuated by his turn to drink, and his stories were all timed to end at the exact moment the last drop of wine was drained from the bottle.

After he'd made sure that we didn't have money to chip-in for another bottle of wine, he'd suddenly remember a pressing engagement and a bunch of important people waiting for him. "You guys have kept me long enough," he'd say, as if great decisions awaited his attention, "and I'm already late." He'd pat each of us on the shoulder and politely thank us for the drink. Then he'd stagger off, shuffling his way up the middle of the street, going back the way he had come, disappearing into the early night.

It was while drinking with Noonie that we boys learned about romance and sex. He taught us "ways with women— what to say to them, how to respect them, and how to love them." He'd scratch diagrams on the ground to illustrate the miracle of reproduction, and once he even stopped drinking until his explanation about the use of contraceptives was clearly understood by each of us. His instructions were explicit but never lurid or disrespectful toward women. Noonie went to great lengths to help us understand that women were to be honored as the wellspring from which all life comes. "You can't call yourself a brother, if you disrespect a sister," he said. "Our manhood is nothing unless we pay homage to their womanhood."

Although we suspected that much of what Noonie said was tailored to fit the occasion, to keep the bottle moving around the circle and back to him, he was the only person in the neighborhood whom we could ask questions about sex. True or false, his answers were all we had, and his words were our gospel.

Noonie's discourses weren't limited to sex. He was a fantastic generalist with a particular interest in African-American history. He often said, "You gotta know who you are, and where you came from, before you can know where you're going and what you want outta life." He'd never mix jokes, slang or jive-talk with history. These were the only times I can ever remember him to be serious. His voice would become soft, almost preachy, sort of like when Reverend Martin delivered a sermon, and though his speech was slurred from drinking, his words were nevertheless easily understood.

It was while standing in the circle drinking wine with Noonie that we learned about Crispus Attucks, a black man who was the first to die in the Boston Massacre, Nat Turner and Denmark Vesey, Toussaint L'Ouverture, Frederick Douglass and John Brown—who Noonie said was really a black man in disguise. He told us stories about Harriet Tubman, Sojourner Truth and Mary McLeod Bethune. He hummed the music of Duke Ellington, Billie Holliday, Lester Young, Charlie Parker and Miles Davis. He quoted from Richard Wright, Zora Neal Hurston, Langston Hughes, James Baldwin and Gwendolyn Brooks. Noonie said they and many others were saints to be remembered and praised.

He breathed life and meaning into the black mountain men, explorers and trail blazers who opened the West; the buffalo soldiers who fought the Indians and black cowboys who rode the Chisholm Trail. "Hollywood tells lies," Noonie said. "They make it seem like black people never existed."

This was both a gripe and a warning. He inspired us to question the roles we saw portrayed in films.

Noonie never drank while he talked about African-American history. He'd hold the bottle close to his chest while he talked, but when he finished talking—look out!—he'd turn the bottle up to his lips and we'd have to scramble to yank it down.

From time to time throughout my teenage years, Noonie would disappear for a week or two, sometimes longer. When he'd return, word would buzz around the neighborhood: "Noonie's back." And the first Saturday evening after his return, we boys would be waiting for him under the streetlight at the corner of the playground.

Noonie never told us where he'd been, and we never asked, but it was rumored that his absence had been ordered by a judge who'd sent him to the county workhouse to sober up. Of course, we never believed those rumors. That was grown-up gossip intended to discredit Noonie. We boys knew the truth. There wasn't a judge alive who had the courage or legal right to sentence our avenger to hard labor in the workhouse.

During one of Noonie's absences, my family moved out of the neighborhood and all the way across the state. I went to a new school and made new friends. Later, after a tour in the Army, I moved to the city where I slipped into a fast, hustling lifestyle and forgot about Noonie.

I was in prison when word filtered through the walls that he had died. He was found dead in a rundown hotel room. He had choked on his own vomit. An empty white port wine bottle was clutched in one hand, and a bottle of lemon juice lay on the floor next to his bed. Noonie went out the way he lived—with a bottle in his hand.

"Good old Noonie," I sighed, "he was a thoroughbred

wino." I pushed the memory of Noonie back into my mind and looked around the prison yard for Willie Neckbone and Wizard. They were leaning against each other for support and watching a chess game at a table near the gym door. It was clear to everyone in the yard that they were drunk; even the guards knew. "No," I thought as I got up from my bench and headed toward the cell block, "Willie Neckbone and Wizard aren't at all like Noonie." Drinking for them was an excuse. They had turned to drink because they couldn't handle prison sober. "Drinking is not their religion," I said to myself. "Not at all like Noonie. They're not willing to die drunk."

Silky

They took Silky away.

Overnight, Silky claimed he'd had a revelation. Said he saw a vision pasted to the wall of his cell: A nude woman with azure eyes, walking on water, stopping only here and there to improvise a few steps of boogie woogie.

When the guards unlocked his cell, Silky stumbled out. He was draped in a blanket; his mug was painted magic marker colors and he proclaimed himself a Seminole Indian Chief, the last direct descendant of that warrior race.

Of course, the guards did not believe a word he said. They never had before. Still, they took him seriously enough not to take any chances.

Silky was rushed to the psych's "space station" and logged into a quiet blue room.

The psych judged Silky to be "non-crazy"—at least not any more crazy than is normal in prison. He read the guard's report, frowned and determined that Silky had not broken any rules. Still, the psych—not one to take a chance—prescribed daily Thorazine, a multitude of muscle relaxants, and ordered an around-the-clock watch on Silky's actions.

In prison, not even the psychiatrist will make allowances for a prisoner changing his history and making his own kind of escape.

◆

Release

In prison, memories become hope.
And hope becomes an absolute trap.
Yet to do nothing is treacherous.

Skeeter Mack's Prison

SKEETER MACK, WHO HAD SURVIVED head-on collisions with self-inflicted madness, switchblades and poison, hair dyes and niggers—both black and white, rattlesnake bites, flat-back hookers, Mad Dog wine and sudden wealth, refused as fact that his only options were to become an expert at gin rummy and a grandmaster at mail-order chess.

In the old days, when Skeeter Mack walked the prison yard, even the redneck guards called him Mr. Nigger. This was at a time when everyone else was just plain, ordinary, everyday nigger. Skeeter Mack deserved that kind of respect.

As times changed, the nature of crimes and the kinds of criminals changed. Skeeter Mack withdrew from the bustle of the main yard into a tight corner of older cronies who stationed themselves in the smaller side yard.

Skeeter Mack said that his withdrawal was a shield to guard against the poetic glibness of the new breed prisoner who buffed their shit like dance hall wax and polished their acts like whores on perpetual stroll.

One spring day following the equinox, while brushing off a hustle—a game played on his spirit—Skeeter Mack reached out and damaged the eyes, lips and rib cage of the popcorn pimp who confronted him.

Skeeter Mack was instantaneously reclassified and listed as a "free-lance lunatic." Six months later he was paroled after being processed through a psychiatric door. He was certified cured but lame-brained.

Convinced by the system that poachers make the best game wardens, Skeeter Mack took a night watchman's job. He oversaw a fancy graveyard and other active stables of *nouveau riche* liberals who prided themselves on hiring an ex-con.

He arranged his sleeping hours so that he would have ample time each day to patrol the parking lot directly across from the prison gate. He watched the gate—alone, bedraggled, cronyless—like a spent horse homesick for the stable. A beached sailor watching the sea.

Each day at shift change time, Skeeter Mack would exchange greetings and assorted niceties with the guards and other workers coming to and leaving the prison. He even had a kind word for the warden. The only person he would not speak to, wave to, or share a nod with, was the psychiatrist. He blamed the psychiatrist for disrupting his prison life by suggesting parole and forcing freedom on him.

While on station in the parking lot, Skeeter Mack would relive his prison memories. His memories were as elaborate as the creations of the Ringling Brothers or Salvador Dali. He remembered every prison face, every prison joke and the hard times too. Although he was alone, his memories of prison kept him company.

One day, two wise-ass jitterbugs approached him. They were fooled by their anger and leaped at Skeeter Mack. The youngsters mistook him for a weak old man, but Skeeter Mack, who often said, "I ain't got this far in life by being no victim," refused to allow them to beat knots on his skull.

When the ambulance arrived at the nearest hospital, the two angry jitterbugs were tagged and slid into an icebox to await their next of kin.

Skeeter Mack refused to plead self-defense, even refused

to give details of the attack so that the court-appointed attorneys could help him. Instead, he copped out to the DA's offer and left the courtroom in chains.

Once again Skeeter Mack sits in the tight corner of older cronies. Now he happily shares memories of his night watchman days, real steak dinners and the yield of a woman's soft flanks. His cronies glue their minds to his every word—a ledge from which to view the outside world, a link between the past and the future. Skeeter Mack has been where every prisoner dreams of going.

Still, when the work shifts change, Skeeter Mack stands near the entrance gate—this time, inside looking out. He smiles as he welcomes the guards and others to another day's work. He even welcomes the warden to what he calls "Skeeter Mack's prison." The warden, of course, chuckles in an understanding way and thanks Skeeter Mack for the welcome.

Although he is now deemed "clinically safe" and reclassified a "resident lunatic," the psychiatrist is still the only one with whom Skeeter Mack will not speak. He turns his back whenever the psychiatrist comes to work. But in the tight corner, in the smaller yard, Skeeter Mack confides to his oldest cronies that his greatest fear is that the psychiatrist will force freedom on him again.

Big Red

When Big Red the Greek arrived in prison, his first act was to cut off all outside contacts. This included his wife and his girl friend, and his woman and even his woman's woman.

Then Big Red the Greek sat down and waited to be released.

Seatrain

"Why are you packing all that junk?" I asked Seatrain who was to be released the next day.

He was busy stuffing stacks of prison rulebooks, regulations, directives and bulletins outlining every aspect of a prisoner's expected conduct into a large cardboard box.

"When I get home," Seatrain said, "I'm gonna put this stuff on the walls of my walk-in closet. And anytime I get the urge to do wrong, I'm gonna smoke a joint and lock myself into that closet and just sit and look at all this shit. Then, I'm gonna ask myself, 'Do you really want to risk going through this again?'" He threw in a handful of laundry tickets, mess hall menus, hobby permits, passes and other prison paraphernalia, closed the box and tied it shut with a rope. "I figure that after about ten seconds of reliving this place, any wrongdoing urges I might have will be gone."

"I can dig it," I said. "That's rehabilitation."

"No, man," Seatrain looked around at the steel walls, the cold water sink, the toilet that seldom worked, the narrow cot and the cell bars. "That's just common sense."

I reminded him that common sense ain't so common.

"Maybe not," he said, "but I sure got it."

He dragged the packed box from his cell and I helped him carry it to the outside gate.

◆

"Rehabilitation is a hoax," Tripe, the guard sergeant, stated. "Don't waste your time on such trivia."

I was dumbfounded.

"A strong image is needed for rehabilitation to work," the sergeant said. "I am the strongest here, but I wouldn't want anyone remade in my image."

I nodded in agreement and received a seven-day disciplinary lockup for insulting an officer by assent.

Roland

"My daddy ain't here." Roland lay awake, looking up into the blackness of his cell and remembering how he was instructed to answer the door when bill collectors came looking for his father. *"My daddy is gone. He won't be home until tomorrow."*

If a bill collector returned the next day and again asked for Roland's father, Roland said, *"He's at the store."* Roland remembered how careful he was not to open the door too wide and how he kept the bill collectors from looking inside.

Now when the bill collectors come, Roland's son has the job of saying, *"My father is not available. I believe he has returned to his place of birth in the South."* If the bill collector persists, Roland's son is instructed to say, *"My daddy has gone forever. He swam back to* Af-free-ca!"

Cold Duck

Cold Duck had served twenty-two years behind the wall, and was soon to go free. That's all that mattered. He had geared his life to this point in time. Each tick of the clock was one second less he would have to stay here, and each step carried him closer to the street door. For the last five years, he had kept his nose clean. He had no rule infractions, not even a notice for an overdue book from the library. Now that there was a light at the end of his tunnel, Cold Duck dreamed about being free.

A hard-ass guard, fresh from the academy, out to make a cheap reputation, called Cold Duck a faggot. Cold Duck shook it off.

The guard smashed a matchstick house which had taken Cold Duck three years to build. Cold Duck swept up the pieces, and thought about his freedom.

Not even the angry tears, which rushed into Cold Duck's eyes when the guard implied that his dead mother had been a whore, could blot out the light in his tunnel. Cold Duck had waited too long to see that light. Now nothing could turn it off.

The more hostile the guard acted, the more passive Cold Duck became. At night Cold Duck prayed: "Please, Dear God, don't let me kill again."

On the morning of the day that Cold Duck was released, the guard stepped in front of him and blocked his path to the door.

"It's too late now," Cold Duck smiled, as he looked past the guard to the outside world. "You're a defeated man," Cold Duck proclaimed.

The guard pulled himself straight, and mock pride covered his pasty face. He opened his mouth to speak, but Cold Duck cut him off.

"You've tried everything you know to break me," Cold Duck said, "but I won't give you a reason to keep me here. I've beaten you at your own game." Cold Duck's voice was a whisper, yet as cold as the steel cell he had survived. "Now," he said, "the least you can do is to stand aside and let a free man go free."

The guard wept. From that day on, the guard was known as a punk.

Banana

I'd been sick, but I'm all right now. Three guards took me out to the county hospital. This was the first time I'd been outside the walls in nearly fifteen years. The last time was when I went to court to hear a judge uphold my conviction without bothering to give a reason. Callous, but legal.

I was in the hospital for five days. Something I'd eaten had given me a blistering rash under my arms, on my forehead, in the folds of my groin, down the small of my back, across my buttocks and behind my knees. The doctors did all sorts of tests and tried a number of medications before they'd let me out of the hospital. I didn't mind being there. It was great to be away from this place, and to be treated like something other than a dog.

In the hospital I was fed good food that had not been boiled down to tasteless mush. I drank fresh milk and even ate real eggs, but the biggest treat was fresh fruit. These are small things to someone not in prison, but for me they were luxuries. Except for an occasional apple, or a shriveled orange, this was my first fresh fruit in more than five years.

How many people have explored the simple pleasure of eating a banana?

When I was given a banana with my first hospital breakfast, I couldn't believe my eyes. It took me a while to realize what I was looking at. It was surreal! Existential! Quintessential! Something worth cheering about! So flawless, in fact, I thought at first it was an imitation—the plastic creation of a pop-artist that had been placed on my breakfast tray for decoration, something to look at, but not to be eaten.

Even after I touched it and discovered it was a real banana, I still hesitated before eating it. I feared a setup. Years of fine-tuning my prison survival instinct for self-preservation convinced me it was a trap set by my guards. They had nothing better to do with their time than to punish me for eating something that wasn't meant for me to enjoy.

Such are the torments of prison life. Even in the hospital, safely away from the source of terror, fears are hard to overcome—seldom do we ever get rid of them.

I finally found the courage to pick up the banana. As I stroked it, I prepared myself for whatever the guards might do to me. It was worth the risk. Never in memory had I felt anything so smooth, so perfect to the touch. And the aroma was intoxicating!

I carried the banana to the window and sat mesmerized by the beauty of its radiant yellow in the morning sunlight. I was overcome with quiet excitement. It was as if I was seeing a banana for the first time after a lifetime of hearing great and wondrous stories about them.

And when I peeled it, taking my time to carefully remove the skin from the pulp, I was doubly amazed. It was beyond my imagination. Nothing in memory hinted at the muted creamy color I uncovered. I had discovered a new world.

Then I sat in the middle of the bed, legs crossed like a buddha, and slowly ate the banana, each bite no more than a nibble. This could well be my last banana for five years, so I wanted to miss nothing. My brain recorded the event in detail. I was determined to recall the experience in full when I was returned to prison and again locked in a dark cell. The memory would be my comforter.

No one has explored the pleasures of a banana more thoroughly. The experience was both aesthetic and erotic, far better than any sex I can remember. I nibbled slowly, deliberately, counting each chew, basking in the taste as the banana was masticated from firm pulp into liquified goo which I oozed through my teeth and squished against the roof of my mouth with my tongue before letting it ease down my throat.

It took me more than an hour to eat the banana. And when I finished, I carefully wrapped the skin in a paper napkin. I planned to savor its aroma later in the night.

As I was about to tuck the wrapped peel under my pillow, the nurse came in to give me a new medication prescribed by the doctor. She saw what I was doing and asked me why I had wrapped the banana peel in the napkin and why I was putting it under my pillow. She did not demand an answer, as I expected she would, as I had become accustomed to in prison. Instead, her voice was gentle, filled with curiosity and compassion. Her concern made me ashamed of my paranoia.

I stuttered as I explained why I was saving the banana peel.

She at first appeared confused, uncertain whether or not to take me seriously. Then she smiled. It was the kind of smile that comes just before a burst of laughter, when the punch line of a good joke hits home. But as my words sank in, her expression changed. Her smile flattened, her eyes misted, and she looked concerned and sad. Not for me, not for herself, but saddened by the situation that linked us in that moment.

She gently touched the back of my hand. "In this hospital," she whispered, her voice soft as dandelions, "you can have a banana with breakfast every morning."

She wiped tears from her eyes and walked out of the room.

◆

"I'm in prison as punishment," Mondongo said, "not *for* punishment. So don't take your hostilities out on me."

The Woman on My Wall

"Do you have fantasies?" Her voice a wind chime; tinkles come from everywhere at once and fill my small chamber.

I finish my pre-bedtime chores and turn toward her.

Her full, cushiony lips are freshly moistened as roses are with dew and partially open in a smile.

"You do have fantasies, don't you?"

Her dark, almond-shaped eyes are wide with interest and follow as I move.

I sit on my cot and gaze back at her. My eyes follow the plush oval curve of high, firm breasts tipped with erect nipples, her tapered waist, the smooth, slow roll of her stomach disappearing into the V of her thighs, thighs slightly parted and framing her pink blossomed vulva nestled in downy angel hair. Her high formed *mons veneris* captures my attention. Even her toes stir my libido.

She is my mandala.

She is my sanctuary.

We walk a wood path down a gentle slope toward an afternoon beach. The air smells of lilacs and violets and feels velvet against my skin. Birds chirping high in the canopy of leaves herald us as trumpets do prince and princess. Smooth, white, crystalline sand spreads before us, welcoming our footprints as lovers do each other's hand. At water's edge, we shed our garments and naked, save for sun rays and Eros' smile, hand in hand we ease into warm water.

We make love on a wave. Rejuvenated. We are washed ashore to lay side by side upon the sand. Nature kisses us with a breeze, sanctifying our union.

Later, after snacks of wine and cheese, fruit and nectar,

we sprawl in each other's arms whispering secrets too dear to be spoken aloud, kissing and feeling the earth quake and move. Then we rejoin love-making.

By starlight we softly say how strange it is that people make war and we fall asleep feeling free and nice and natural things against our skins.

"Yes, I have fantasies," I admit to the woman smiling at me. "At one time, I had memories, but they are all gone now."

"Are your fantasies of me?" Nightingales are shamed by her voice.

The night bell clangs, ringing to end another day. The uniformed guard halts before my cell door. He peers in through the bars.

"Jay," the guard says, then calls me by my prison nickname. "Sheetrock, were you talking to yourself again?" His tone is as impersonal as the "thank you" of a meat market clerk.

I continue to stare at the enchantress before me.

"Were you talking to yourself again?" He repeats his question, this time a bit harsher for being ignored.

"Yes," I force myself to say, "I suppose I was talking to myself."

"Don't let it get to you," the guard says as he moves on along the corridor of cells, completing his nightly head count.

"Don't let it get to you" is the same thing he has said to me every night for the last five years.

The programmed routineness is debilitating and treacherous. It affects both the watcher and the watched.

Soon the lights will be turned off and another lonely night will settle in. There is never a change, except that which occurs within my mind.

I lean across the narrow cell space and lightly kiss the

mouth of the woman smiling out from the magazine centerfold pasted to my cell wall.

She is my confidante.

She is my escape.

"Yes," I say to her, "my fantasies are of you."

"Please tell them to me," she cajoles as I lay down to
monologue myself to sleep.

The return of the prison-grey morning comes too soon.

Little Danny Lomax

Little Danny Lomax took a knife to the hospital. It was
buried in his chest.

Eyewitnesses said that Danny had slipped and fallen
while cleaning his toenails.

The only fingerprints found on the knife were Danny's
where he had tried to un-stick himself before giving up the
ghost. But rules are rules and the official investigator had no
choice except to charge Danny with "homicide of self" and
"destroying State property." At the bottom of the "unusual in-
cident" report, the investigator wrote: "Little Danny Lomax.
Former prisoner. Released by sudden death."

A Bright Spot in the Yard

Jomo was laughing to himself when I first saw him
standing with his back pressed against the brick building at
one side of the exercise yard. His clean-shaven head was tilted
back on his short neck, his moon face glistened with sweat
and his eyes were fixed on a point in the sky, high above the
prison's grey walls.

"Him's really a strange piece of God's work," Spokane

Mack spoke through his straight-across-the-face mouth and nodded toward Jomo as he, Tankcar and I walked the yard.

Tankcar hunched his huge shoulders and pulled down the corners of his lips in a way that made the razor scar on his cheek stand out in bas relief. "A bona fide *nut*," Tankcar said, emphasizing the word "nut." "Some guys never recover from the trauma of being arrested."

I looked at Jomo out of the corners of my eyes. His eyes were wide. Staring. Entranced. Columbus sighting the New World; Moses looking into the Promised Land. I rubbed my hand down across my chin, remembered I hadn't shaved in two days and asked, "What's his trip?"

"Too many years behind the walls," Spokane Mack said. "Now him's on everybody's pay-him-no-mind list."

"That's his spot in the yard," Tankcar informed me. "Nobody ever stands there but Jomo."

I said it was a damn shame the way prison could do a person and vowed never to let it happen to me.

"Anybody's number can play," Tankcar reminded me.

As days eased into weeks and weeks into months, Jomo became more of an accepted fixture in the yard than a fellow prisoner, sort of like the guardposts. He'd be there on his spot when I'd come out into the yard and he'd be the last one to leave when we were ordered back to our cells at night. Sometimes I wondered about him, and a few times even felt sorrow, but, like other prisoners, I had my own problems and seldom paid him any attention until the day he materialized at my elbow and asked for a match.

I handed him a book of matches.

He stared at the matches.

"Is there anything wrong?"

He turned his eyes on me. "Where's the cigarette?" he asked, then smiled.

It was the kind of smile that went all the way around his neck and showed a lot of pretty teeth. His eyes were glossy but not fixed in a crazed stare. Still, I stepped back, put a little more space between us and rested my hand on the eight-inch length of steel pipe I had rolled into a magazine and tucked into my hip pocket. In prison, where paranoia and violence determine the life style, I intended not to be a victim—especially not of someone who everybody knew to be a nut.

I kept my eyes on him. "What cigarette?" I asked.

His smile didn't change. "The one that you are about to give me," he said, then looked off into the sky as if searching for his next words. He found them and said, "I would look very, very silly striking a match with no cigarette to smoke." He smiled at me some more. "Now, wouldn't I?" he asked.

I studied his face for telltale signs of lunacy. I couldn't find any. He was just another guy dealing with prison life in the best way he could. There was nothing insane about that. I relaxed my grip on the steel pipe and handed him my pack of cigarettes.

He shook one free of the pack. "You're unlike the others here."

"How's that?"

He returned the pack of cigarettes and rolled the one he had kept between his fingers. His hands were large, had a lot of small scars on them. They were clean with the nails trimmed close.

"You still trust." His tone told me that he was about to make his point. I waited. He hung the cigarette in his lips, lit it, blew a slow puff of smoke, then said, "This place hasn't burned the trust out of you yet."

"That's an awful lot to read into one cigarette," I said.

He smiled again. This time not as wide as before. Still it was a good smile, not a pasted-on deception. "If you didn't trust," he said, "you wouldn't have let me have your full pack."

I saw his point. I hadn't been in prison long enough to know all the ropes. I made a mental note to go along with the pipe in my back pocket.

"Actions tell the story." He blew more smoke and winked at me. Then, as an afterthought, he said, "As we get to know each other, I'll share my secrets with you."

"Secrets?" I leaned back a little and gave him one of those long looks meant to imply doubt.

"Yeah," he nodded. The sun bounced off his head as he moved it up and down. "Real secrets."

I gave him another doubtful look.

His face became serious. He caught my arm and pulled me closer.

I yanked free.

He leaned in on me and whispered, "I know how to escape this place."

I froze. I stared at him. My heart tried to pound a hole in my chest. Sweat rushed down my armpits. The words caught in my throat and I had to kick them out. "Escape? How?" The words trembled out like a knock-kneed school girl on her first date.

He smiled again. He knew that he had me. "In time," he whispered as he blew some smoke, then watched it drift away. "In time you'll get all the answers." Then he changed up, as if someone had called him from across the yard. "Right now, I have to go visit with a friend."

Jomo dropped the cigarette, crushed it out, turned on his heels and walked off. He kept his head high and rolled on the balls of his feet. A few guys saw him coming and moved out of his way. Instead of going into one of the cell blocks where his friend might be, he went directly across the yard to

his spot, stood with his back to the building and turned his
face to the sky.

I saw Jomo every day. Still, it was another two weeks before we spoke again.

I was coming from the mess hall when he fell in beside
me and said, "To understand that some people don't understand is to be called insane."

I didn't bother asking him to explain. There was only
one thing I wanted to know—how to escape.

"When you're ready," he said.

"Hell," I nearly shouted, "I'm ready to go now."

"You only think that you're ready." He turned and
started away.

I called after him.

He stopped and looked back at me.

I took a step toward him, but he held up his hand, sig-
naling me to a halt.

"I have a party invitation." He grinned. "And I never
want to be late." He flicked a parting wave and crossed the
yard to his spot against the brick building.

I was left standing in the middle of the yard like a man
waiting for something to happen; nothing did. Jomo spent the
rest of the afternoon standing on his spot in the yard and staring up.

The next morning I caught up with Jomo as he came
from his cell block. He seemed depressed. His shoulders
drooped and his head hung like a melon on a vine. The luster
was gone from his face and his eyes were recessed and dull as
if he hadn't slept. I spoke to him, but he rushed past and hurried on to his spot.

No sooner had Jomo braced his back against the building and turned his face to the sky, his depression started to

lift. It was a transformation. His shoulders squared themselves. The deep-rooted smile returned, his face gleamed as if
polished and his eyes became full and round and alive with
the excitement of a faithful worshipper witnessing a miracle.
He started to giggle. Then he laughed aloud. Tears came from
his eyes and those who passed shook their heads and gave
him plenty of room.

"Why you hanging with that nut?" Tankcar asked as he
and Spokane Mack eased up on me.

Tankcar's prison shirt was cut off at the sleeves and the
seams were busted under the arms. His muscles were still
pumped up and sweaty from working out on the weight pile.
He was one of the best weightlifters in the joint. Spokane
Mack rocked on his heels. He was cleaning his fingernails and
chewing on a toothpick.

"The man ain't nuts," I said.

"Shit he ain't." Tankcar wiped a line of sweat from his
face.

"Him's a space case," Spokane said. "Look at him."

Jomo was hysterical with laughter. His eyes were riveted
on a spot high in the sky, focused as if watching a comedy. He
was a mesmerized child.

Spokane laughed and said, "Better watch yourself. That
loony stuff is catching."

"Yeah, man," Tankcar put in, "you'd better check your
role."

I looked over at Jomo. He was in his own world, his own
space, his own time zone. He wasn't in prison; he wasn't anyplace, at least not any place that I knew anything about.

Spokane Mack put his nail file away, checked his nails to
see how good a job he had done, then said, "In this place, it
don't take much to end up like him is."

I thought about it for a moment, thought some more,

then thought about escaping, then said, "I can handle it."

"Suit yourself," Tankcar said. He nodded to Spokane and said, "Come on. Let's walk."

They glanced at Jomo, then went on around the yard. I took the magazine from my hip pocket. The steel pipe felt heavy rolled in the magazine. I watched Jomo for a few seconds more. Then I went looking for a place to sit and read.

Jomo spent the next two hours staring into the sky and laughing to himself before coming over to where I sat reading. I was sitting on a small bench in the shade of the corner where two of the cell blocks came together. From there I had a full view of the yard. It was a three ring circus of inmates busy getting through another prison day.

A full tilt basketball game rushed up and down the asphalt court. Handball matches happened against one wall. Teams were being picked for volleyball. A softball game was warming up and men hunched at tables playing cards, chess and checkers. Off to one side, strong men worked in the flat sunlight, lifting iron weights. Runners, in tandems of five, jogged around the perimeter of the yard to a cadence called on every fourth step . Two prison queens lounged near the chapel door and guards kept watch while slick-kids and prison hustlers stalked their next victims. Only Jomo was alone and stood still.

Now he was standing before me, smiling.

"Some people will put anything into their heads," Jomo said as he looked down at me.

I slid over to make room for him.

"They'll fill their heads with shit," he said, "just to have something there." Then he asked for a cigarette.

I offered him the pack.

He smiled. "Still haven't changed," he said and took one without taking the pack from my hand. He dug into his pants' pocket, found a match, lit the cigarette, then apologized for ignoring me earlier.

"I had to clear my head." He leaned back and looked off into the sky. "The guy who locks in the cell next to mine thinks that prison is a game. He kept talking and yelling all night. I didn't sleep at all."

I agreed that one of the worst things about being in prison is not having a choice of who's around you.

Jomo puffed the cigarette and flicked the ash on the ground between his feet. "He's out of touch with himself," he said, "and because he doesn't realize the danger of this place, he's a danger to others."

I thought of all the prisoners who had been brutalized, and of the ones who had died. "It takes all kinds," I said as I adjusted the steel pipe to keep it from sliding out from under my shirt where I had it tucked. "We can't do each other's time here, but we can do it together."

On the basketball court an argument erupted over a doubtful score. A knot of angry inmates gathered under one basket and their voices got loud. The inmate referee rushed in and got the game moving again. The team managers were satisfied; the players were satisfied; the spectators were satisfied; and the guard in the guntower unloaded his weapon and replaced it in the rifle rack.

"Everyone here is a walking time bomb," I said.

"Some aren't," he said. "There's a few of us who have learned to keep our peace." He glanced sideways at me.

"It's the fucked-up ones." I thought of a shitload of guys who made it their business to make life hard for others.

"That's what happened to me." Jomo dropped the cigarette butt and crushed it with the toe of his brogans. "My cell neighbor broke my peace last night. So, first thing this morning, I had to clean his crap from my head." He took a deep breath, then didn't say anything for a long time. When he spoke, he said, "I know that you understand."

I said that I understood the necessity of clearing his head but I didn't understand how he went about it. This led us into a conversation about interplanetary visitations and psychic phenomena and telepathy and even how the uniform grey of the prison is a well-ordered scheme to neutralize and control us. We agreed that everything was possible, nothing was to be discounted.

I slipped the steel pipe from under my shirt and rolled it back into the magazine, then slid the tight packet into my hip pocket. Jomo saw the pipe but said nothing.

Jomo tipped his head back and looked up at the sky. Fluffy white clouds stacked on top of each other like puffs of cotton candy were moving in over the prison. He studied the clouds for a long time as if making something of them. Then he brought his head down and said, "I'll answer your questions."

How to escape was the only question I had, but instead of asking that question, I asked why was he always watching the sky.

He laughed, but it really wasn't a laugh. It was more like a little chuckle that caused him to squint his eyes. "You're the first person to ever ask me that," he said. "Fact is, you're the first person in years to really talk with me."

From the way that others avoided him, I knew this to be true. Still I wanted to know his reasons for standing on that spot and looking at the sky, especially when he had said that he knew how to escape. So I asked him again.

He looked around to be sure that no one was close enough to overhear. Then he whispered, "The secret of that spot is dynamite."

"Hold it, Jomo," I said. "Don't take me on a trip. Just give it to me straight."

"This is straight." He nodded his head slowly up and down. "If it were known just how powerful the secret is, the guards would make that spot off limits and no one would be able to go there ever again."

Perhaps everything I'd heard about Jomo was right. Perhaps he was nuts after all. Perhaps I was a bit wacky, too, for believing he wasn't. But there was that outside chance that, crazy or not, Jomo did know how to get out of the prison. I had to take that chance.

"A secret place, huh?" I said, going along with him.

He nodded his head again.

I looked across the yard to his spot by the brick building. There was nothing there. Then I looked at the drab greyish-brown cell block buildings, then to the high sandy-grey wall with its peaked roof guntowers, then around the yard again and back to his spot. There was still nothing there. I could see nothing secret about it. It was just a little open space next to a prison building. On the contrary, if anything, it was conspicuous. It was at the most exposed point in the whole yard and I was sure that nothing covert could possibly happen there without every eye seeing it.

"What's so secret about being in the open?" I asked.

He hunched his shoulder, thought it over, then relaxed and said, "Some of the best kept secrets are in the open." His voice had an air of intrigue like a man making up riddles for others to solve. I could tell that he was having fun. "In the open," he went on, "no one ever bothers trying to find them."

A guard patrolling the yard ambled by. The guard tried to appear nonchalant but we knew his job was to watch and listen. We stopped talking until the guard had passed.

"Skeptics always fall the hardest. Come on." He bounced up from the bench and took me by the arm. "I'll show you."

He pulled me. I had to jog to keep from being dragged as he led me past knots of talking inmates and across the yard.

"You won't need that pipe in your hind pocket anymore," Jomo said.

And I was suddenly aware of the weight of the pipe pulling my right hip down. It contrasted with the lightness of Jomo's hand on my arm.

"After today," he said as a group of four inmates got out of our way, "no one will bother with you again." He chuckled and added, "They probably won't even talk to you."

The four inmates eyed us as if we were contagious. I looked at them. Each turned his eyes away as if afraid that I would speak to him. I dropped the pipe, still wrapped in the magazine, into a garbage can as Jomo hurried me past and we came to his spot in the yard.

"I've never brought anyone here," Jomo said as we stopped. "Before I show you anything, you'll have to swear not to tell a soul until the right time."

He looked me in the eyes, then studied my face. He was as careful as a lockpicker. I felt that each pore in my skin was being scrutinized under a magnifying glass.

I mouthed a promise without the slightest thought that one day I'd be bound to keep and protect it.

"I got this spot from an old con everybody called Crazy Billy." His voice was low, as smooth as a golfer's stroke and each word was clearly spoken as if he was passing on something that should be remembered. "That was years back. This was his spot. He was always here and everybody thought that he was really crazy. He just had another way of seeing things, that's all. When the time was right, Crazy Billy brought me here and showed me this spot."

The guard making his rounds of the yard slowed, glanced at us, and walked on.

After the guard was out of earshot, I asked what happened to Crazy Billy.

"Gone."

"Escaped?"

"No," Jomo said, then chuckled. It was the kind of chuckle you get when a person is enjoying an inside joke and you're left standing flatfooted and wondering what it's all about. "Crazy Billy escaped every day," he said, "but when it came time to leave, they released him."

He was inventing riddles again, words with double meanings. I didn't even try to understand.

"From this spot," Jomo said, "the prison disappears."

I was just as confused as before but this time I let out a somewhat doubtful "What?" I looked at the ground, then surveyed the yard. Nothing had changed. Everything was just as it always had been: A prison.

Jomo was grinning. He was very pleased with himself. After he had checked to be sure that no one was nearby, he explained, "This is the only spot where you can stand and see nothing of the prison at all."

Around the yard the cell blocks with rusting window bars were still there. The watch posts and the uniformed guards were still there. The games inmates played were still going on. The sound of a thousand voices was still there. The lowered heads, the hollowed eyes and the shuffling feet were all still there. There was no doubt about it. This was still a prison.

"On this spot," Jomo stopped grinning and his face became solemn—his voice was low and filled with the inner warmth of a priest saying vespers—"you can become a wizard. A sorcerer. You can conjure the spirits of other worlds." His eyes were glossy and went into a far-off fix. "You can visit the infinite. Create passionate and hypnotic unions with the angels. Have affairs with queens, nymphs, concubines and common whores."

He was mesmerized and his words came in a flock, rushing together. He became absorbed in his own rhythm. "You can know the charm of the occult. Wall in the supernatural and make real anything you wish." His rhythm suddenly broke and the words came as a flash flood, then went into a long stammer. "Be sanctified. Supreme. Ubiquitous. Omnipotent. Almighty. Divine. Swifter than Mercury. More powerful than Paris, Mars, Apollo, the Titans, and even Zeus."

He went on talking but I had stopped listening. My hope for an escape had become the charade of a lunatic. I felt sorry for him. I felt sorry for myself. I shook my head and started off.

"You can't leave," Jomo shouted. He grabbed my arm. His eyes were aflame, his jaw was set and his moon face shifted between panic and anger.

"Jomo," I said calmly, facing him square on and trying not to show my disappointment. "You said you'd show me how to escape. Now you're serving me word games."

"You'll be a god," he said.

"I'd rather be free." I took a step to leave.

He slid his hand down to my wrist. I tried to pull away but his fingers were like vise grips and my whole arm ached from the pressure. With his other hand he caught the front of my shirt. His energy exploded. He lifted me, yanked me around and slammed my back against the brick building. I was stunned. I thought about the steel pipe in the garbage can. It was only a few yards away. I braced my foot against the wall behind me and pushed, but nothing happened. He was planted like Gibraltar at the Straits. I thought of all the stories about lunatics and their superhuman strength and looked around for help.

"You will be free." Jomo's mouth was close to my ear. He bit each word off so that it came hard and evenly spaced.

Out of the corner of my eye I caught a glimpse of the guard starting toward us.

Jomo released my wrist and brought that hand up under my chin. He forced my head up, high, then back hard until my eyes were on the sky.

The sky.

Jomo was right.

The prison disappeared.

It was only when I was able to turn or lower my head slightly against the pressure of Jomo's hand that the prison came into view. Otherwise, there was only the open sky dotted with fluffy, slow moving clouds riding eastbound zephyrs. The guard never came. Now there was no reason for him to come. I relaxed and the weight of the prison was gone. I was a caterpillar suddenly transformed into a beautiful butterfly.

Jomo felt the change in me and relaxed his grip but didn't take his hands away. "Because you've been looking for the devious," he whispered into my ear, "you've failed to see the obvious."

I felt a smile forming. It came from a long time ago. From the other side of grief and sorrow. From my youth. From innocence. From the days when I had nothing to worry about. The smile struggled up through years of knotted guts, releasing tensions and relieving the pall and paranoia of prison as it came. Then it was there, spreading my lips back tight across my teeth, taking root in my face and feeling as if it was the only way ever to feel.

"Your dreams are contraband, but they are your only refuge." Jomo's words were a talisman. His voice was melodic and pure in a way I'd never heard before. He was the Siren luring a willing Ulysses. Only here, deliverance, not destruction, was the reward.

Even when he removed his hand from under my chin, I continued to keep my face to the sky. A herd of fluffy clouds drifted into view and, for the first time, I was aware of a warm breeze against my skin. It was a different breeze than usually blew in the prison yard; this one carried the scent of seaweed with it. As my eyes followed the clouds, the breeze ebbed and took me as it went. I was stretched on a strip of white sand tucked in a fold between rocky cliffs that slanted down and jutted into the sea like the arms of a lonely lover.

"Free yourself," Jomo coaxed. "Your dreams are your only escape."

Saltwater smells filled the air. Waves formed and rolled and foamed and swished and roared onto the beach.

"You can do anything and go anywhere you want."

The same water that Magellan sailed, that drowned Captain Ahab, that floated the Ark, that baptized Jesus, now washed my feet.

"You can be anyone you wish to be and there will be no guards to stop you."

The damp bathing suit cooled my skin and the fine sand was gritty under my back as I lay looking at the sky, counting clouds and choosing one to ride out, then back.

"Look," Jomo said, filled with surprise. "Look there." That cloud. See?" He pointed to a small puff trailing the herd. "That's the same cloud I saw over Kyoto in Japan yesterday."

Now Jomo's cloud was over the flat blonde beach in western Africa where I lay.

"A geisha and I walked in flowers along the Katsura River." Jomo's voice was filled with warm remembrances. "We watched children play and heard doves coo. Later, we sat close and sipped Pearl Dew Tea in the Imperial Villa while the white-faced Kabuki rehearsed."

I lay on a beach towel and marveled at the blend of women around me. They were sunbathing and strolling and swimming—all unashamedly clad in bright-colored wedges of gossamer cloth riding the tight pubic triangles of their dark thighs.

"Then, at sunset," Jomo's voice came from the other side of the world, "we wrote our names with love on that very cloud."

A lone woman gestured. Our eyes met, then smiles came naturally. Her name was the heart of a song. Our hands touched, our minds locked, the earth moved and at that moment, I knew I could walk on water.

"And now," Jomo said, "here comes that cloud again to give me a second chance."

"Yes, Jomo," I said, my voice came trembling from far away. "It comes to give us both a second chance."

From then on, everyday, Jomo and I stood on our spot with our backs against the brick building. Sometimes we would transport each other with whispered visions. At other times we would escape alone, silently watching our visions merge with the sky.

One morning after breakfast, Jomo said as we started across the yard, "They took Spokane last night."

"Spokane Mack?" I asked, not sure what he was talking about.

"Yeah. Took him to the mental hospital," Jomo said. "He lost his grip, couldn't cope any longer and tried to hang-up. The nightwatch cut him down in time."

"Damn shame," I said, then asked, "what happened?"

"He found out that his woman's been shacking with the cop who busted him."

A maintenance gang was busy repairing the façade of a cell block building. One of the gang glanced at us, shook his head, then mumbled something I couldn't understand, nor did I care to know. We stepped around him and went on.

"Suicide is a lonely way to free yourself," Jomo said.

"Never thought that Spokane Mack would crack up."

"When a man outlives his image," Jomo said somewhat philosophically, "and has nothing else, he's bound to crack."

We went on around the basketball court. A game was just getting started. Tankcar came toward us. He looked small, alone and vulnerable without Spokane Mack at his side. His customary swagger was gone; now he moved at a slow shuffle. His head was lowered, his muscles looked flabby and unused and he was mumbling to himself.

Jomo nudged me and whispered, "Word has it that Tankcar's woman is also getting it from a cop."

Tankcar shuffled past. He didn't seem to notice us. His eyes were deep hollows in his face and looked as sad as a fortune teller's fate.

"The biggest danger in prison is the psychological scarring, not the physical," Jomo said as we arrived at our spot.

Three months after my first escape, Jomo was released. We had shared daydreams and through our visions had become friends. Yet on the day he was released from prison, we didn't say good-bye. I was standing against the building, flying with an eagle in the sky.

We flew over the Rocky Mountains, then east, then east some more.

I came to earth in ancient Timbuktu. The tart aroma of fresh camel dung prickled my nostrils as I strolled the baked clay streets to the market square in the shadow of the great Dyinuree Mosque. Senegalese, Bantu and Bambute tradesmen bartered candies and nuts and cheese, spice and dried fruit for salt bricks mined from the pits at Taoudenni. From open-front booths, Songhai merchants sold Arab cloth, Moorish jewelry, and belly dancers born at the mouth of the Nile, while derelicts asked alms and floral-tailed peacocks strutted nearby.

In the dry noon shade of a palm, I sat on a Persian rug, and my feet cooled in the crystal Oasis of Amen-Ra. There I sipped quick-chilled pomegranate juice laced with anisette served by mulatto eunuchs and watched ebony concubines from south of the Sudan parade to the auctioneer's call. That evening, after dining with a nomad prince, I climbed onto a cloud, and looking into the coming night sky, I heard the guard sergeant shout: "Okay, you men. Clear the yard. Get your asses back to your cells."

When I returned to the prison, Jomo had gone.

Now, thirteen years later, I still spend my days standing on my spot in the yard. One day, I'll find a new prisoner to pass my secret to, but for now, I like taking solo flights, drifting wherever I like and escaping in the sky. It's lonely at times, yes, but the greatest thing about being called insane is that no one bothers asking me to explain.

Of course I hear the whispers of the inmates and guards. They all call me a space case and they joke about my clean-shaven head. They've nicknamed me "The Looney Tune." But I'm immune to all that. I don't talk to them and they don't talk to me. And I'm glad they pay me no mind. They have neither dreams nor visions and, therefore, no escape. Their lives are defined by the prison walls.

I am free.

Getting-Out Day

A squad of guards stood near the main gate to watch me leave prison. They were cretins, about as intelligent as kelp, with faces that called to mind the underside of an endive. They stood packed together, dripping random sweat like grease from a picked-over hambone.

They were angry that I was walking out of their prison alive. Their taut, frustrated expressions revealed how badly they failed to work their harness over my head. They consoled each other and took false comfort in the hope that if I didn't return to prison, I would surely send my young to grow old behind their walls.

I gathered up the start of my new, post-prison life, a rumpled brown paper bag stuffed with personal belongings, and the forty dollars allotted to me by the State as "gate money." After more than sixteen years in prison, I trembled when facing the outside world with so little to face it with. A good meal and a bus ride could bankrupt me.

The guards sensed my trepidation. They sniffed it from the air like rabid hounds sniffing fear from their prey. They sneered at me and barbed taunts followed their sneers. They huddled to scheme one last violation of their rules to charge me with before letting me go free.

Their malice only served to focus my attention, riveted my mind to the outside world. I braced myself and walked past them. I was the steer these cowhands could not dog to the ground. And more than ever before, I became determined that their bodies would garnish lonely graves before I again would feed the bowels of their prison with my mother's shame.

Time After Time

STATE OF NEW YORK
EXECUTIVE DEPARTMENT
DIVISION OF PAROLE

FINAL DISCHARGE

Albany, New York   NOVEMBER 1, 1991

This is to certify that   WASHINGTON, JEROME   *has this day been discharged from further jurisdiction of the Board of Parole in accordance with the provisions of law.*

BOARD OF PAROLE

Chairman

Afterword

RETURNING TO AMERICA after living in France, China, Swaziland or the high Himalayas is one thing, but returning to America after serving sixteen years and three months in maximum security is something altogether different.

In 1972 when I went to prison, Nixon was president and politicians were still thought to be ethical; Patti Hearst was involved in a self-kidnapping conspiracy with the SLA; the Supreme Court was reasonably balanced; the Vietnam War was winding down, but the weekly body count was still news. The HIV virus was unknown and free sex had more fans than a Super Bowl game. Although everybody was not living the American Dream, and some people felt that life was hopeless, most were optimistic about their future and many had a strong commitment to social activism. People cared, and even the most disadvantaged could still dream without fear of having nightmares. This was a legacy. It was cultivated during the 1960s and spilled over into the 1970s.

I was still in prison while Reagan was in the White House. Perhaps I was fortunate. When Reagan cut programs for the rest of the nation, prisoners were unaffected. We were already at the bottom of the shit pile where there was nothing left to cut. It didn't matter who was president, we still had to do the time. However, I am curious about what happened in and to America while I was in prison.

Back on the streets, the first thing I notice is the desperation on people's faces. They now seem more paranoid, more isolated and more xenophobic than when America was being defeated in war by a small third world nation and I was a veteran turned anti-war activist.

In front of St. Patrick's Cathedral I realize that the desperation is pervasive. It's on everyone's face. It cuts across class and cultural lines. It stands out in bas relief, the common denominator between old and young, rich and poor. Even when people are having fun, it's there. I even saw it on the face of a baby in his mother's arms. The child was too young to walk, too young to talk, but old enough to express himself. Perhaps, while I was in prison, exiled from society, desperation as a social phenomenon mutated into something genetic, something that is now passed from generation to generation. I wonder if desperation is as rampant in America's bedrooms as it is on America's streets.

I was with my brother Freddy. We were standing at Columbus Circle, a major hub, a New York City crossroads. Freddy was my guide. He asked where I'd like to go; what I'd like to do; what I'd like to see. Did I want to meet new people, or just hang out, drift from place to place? Suddenly, life was a smorgasbord, a cornucopia of enticements and alluring temptations. I didn't know where to start, what to do first. Prison was my immediate reference point and, there, decisions related to physical movement were made by the guards, not by me. Now decisions were mine to make. Impulse told me to do everything. Uncertainty told me to do nothing. The choice was up to me. "We can't stand here all day," my brother said, over and over.

"Go slow," I told myself as I recalled a number of prisoners who shortly after being released returned to prison with new convictions, and new sentences. They tried to make everything happen at once, all at the same time. Like children, they wanted instant gratification. Played all their cards at the same time, swung before the ball got to the plate, struck out and found themselves back in a cell where their only landscape was the sun setting against the prison wall.

After my release from prison, the world presented me with a lot of maybe's and possibilities. It takes time to sort things out, put them into workable categories. Sometimes, while walking on the streets, I feel as though a spaceship left me on the wrong planet. At other times everything seems natural and falls into place. Still, a bit of uncertainty lurks behind everything, everywhere.

I decided to do life the same way I did prison. Nothing fancy. One step at a time, one day at a time, and most of all, don't forget to breathe.

"Let's just hang out," I told my brother, "go with the flow, move with the groove."

Freddy was supportive and sensitive. He understood that I needed to relearn the rhythm of the streets, tune in on the city, explore my new freedom and tune out on prison. I had no preference which direction we'd walk, or which street we'd take. Freddy didn't seem to have any preference either. He just started off, leaving me to stay where I was or to catch up. I learned a quick but important lesson. It was this kind of small, ordinary decision—often taken for granted and overlooked—that I missed most in prison. Now, by just walking off and letting me decide what to do, Freddy was tuning me in again to this level of free choice.

I was a writer, and I went to prison with organizing skills I'd learned and sharpened during the social movements of the sixties. Shortly after arriving in prison, I set up writing workshops and started a newspaper. It was based on the principles of Chinese collective farms where everybody knew every job, and everyone worked for the common good. This was a new concept for prisons. It worked, and the newspaper gained a "respectable" reputation among inmates, and even had a readership outside the prison.

As a writer, editor, teacher and organizer, I became too successful in an otherwise unsuccessful system. My success placed me at risk with guards, officials and others whom I sometimes referred to as "social retards."

When I refused to allow my writings to be used "to further the goals" of the prison system (whatever they could have been), and also refused to become a "cooperative inmate" by informing on others, goon squad guards attempted to intimidate me with threats of bodily harm. But I'd been through all of that in the sixties—overt racists in the deep South; closet racists in the deep North; brick-throwing hawks during the anti-war peace demonstrations, capitalists opposed to anti-poverty campaigns, and cops who didn't like the color of my necktie. I was inured to threats, and a few upstate New York farmers who were mean-spirited enough to qualify as prison guards weren't about to turn me around.

I did what any writer would. I wrote what I knew to be the truth. I didn't snivel, and my words cut close to the bone. The prison system had my body, but not my mind. My thoughts became contraband to guards and officials, and they soon thought of me as a terrorist who could destroy their prison walls with words. The best review I've ever received came from Robert J. Henderson, at the time the warden at New York's Auburn State Prison. He called my writing "venom." I would have been damned by praise if he had said anything less.

Inmate informers—snitches—told the warden that I was teaching "communism" to the newspaper staff, and that I was planning to write a "major exposé" in which the warden and others would be named. After that, it was only a matter of time. Guards and officials conspired to have me transferred to Attica prison—the scene of the 1971 rebellion and massacre in which forty-three unarmed prisoners and hostages were gunned down by prison guards and State Police.

Officials first claimed that I was guilty of "personal criticisms of the prison system, its employees and policies in satirical editorial articles." They stupidly went on to claim that my writings had "caused a great deal of animosity and concern" within the "citizenry" outside the prison walls.

Although most Constitutional rights are stopped at the prison gate, the protections of the First Amendment are not. The official reason for my transfer became a violation of the First Amendment, which protects the right to write as well as the right to free speech.

It was late 1978 when I was shipped to Attica. ("The name rattles my teeth like snakes," a friend wrote to me.) The officials claimed I had been sent to Attica for "reprogramming," which simply meant they intended to silence my voice as a writer. In the process of transferring me (handcuffed and shackled) to Attica, the guards and officials confiscated my typewriter, manuscripts and more than two years of research.

Not only did I continue to write, but I wrote with a vengeance, and I also filed a First Amendment lawsuit in Federal District Court against the warden who had ordered me transferred to Attica.

My intent was simple: Make the officials live by the laws they swore to uphold. By the time the suit came to trial in the summer of 1985, I had been moved from Attica to another maximum security prison—Green Haven, not far from Poughkeepsie, New York.

The lawsuit became a cause. It attracted wide outside attention and support, and threatened to let more light into the

prison system than guards and officials would like. During
the trial, the warden I sued attempted to change the reason for
my transfer to Attica. He now claimed I had been transferred
for "security concerns."

When pressed by my attorneys to explain these "security
concerns," the warden first testified that I had been "improp-
erly" collecting information that linked prison guards to the
KKK. When that failed to stand the test of cross-examination
and to make an impression on the jury, he then claimed that
my writing incited a small riot in which a number of inmates
were injured. That also failed to impress the jury.

In a last ditch effort, the warden claimed to have information (from a "reliable" inmate informer) that I was a "card-
carrying member" of The Black Panthers or The Black
Liberation Army (he couldn't remember which), and that I
was a "deep plant" who had been sent to prison on a special
mission. According to the warden, I was to sit in prison and
wait for the right signal, and then foment riots throughout the
entire prison system. After making a few more improbable at-
tempts to justify "security concerns" as the reason for my
transfer and the confiscation of my typewriter and writings, it
became clear that the warden was a victim of his own mythol-
ogy. In prison, paranoia works both ways. It affects the
watcher as much as it does the watched.

After eight days of trial, the jury returned a verdict in my
favor. This was a major victory. It was the first time such a
case against a prison official had ever been won by a prisoner.
The lawsuit forced prison officials, at least in New York State,
to live by the spirit as well as the letter of the law.

The morning after my release from prison found me in
Harlem. I was staying with Bert, a long-time family friend. I
awoke at dawn. There was no excitement. No stage fright, or

butterflies to signal the first day of the rest of my life. Looking up from sleep I could have dreamt my release from prison the day before. The sky was as grey as a prison sky—the same sky I had seen for the past sixteen years and three months.

I looked out the window, down and across Fifth Avenue. Harlem's Fifth Avenue is not the Fifth Avenue of fashionable mid-town Manhattan. This Fifth Avenue is lined with burned-out and abandoned buildings. It resembles the TV scenes of Beirut I'd seen night after night on the six o'clock news while in prison. Also from the nightly news reports, I expected to see muggings and rapes, murders, pillaging and plundering in broad daylight. Or at least witness the victims of the night's crimes being carted off by sanitation workers. But I saw none of that.

Instead of violence and mayhem, my attention was drawn to a lone school crossing guard. A woman in a dark blue uniform with a broad white belt that slashed down across her left shoulder and went around her waist. She stood on one corner of 132nd Street and Fifth Avenue. She was keeping vigil for neighborhood children. Hers was an act of love. Caring. This was not the Harlem the six o'clock news had led me to expect. Instead, this was ordinary, everyday Harlem, a Harlem I'd been led to believe was nonexistent.

Even the cops appear more paranoid now than years ago. I asked one for street directions. His hand went to his gun. It was a reflex action, and his hand stayed on his gun while he gave me directions which turned out to be incorrect. Later, I got correct directions from a homeless man who was pushing his belongings along the street in a liberated supermarket shopping cart. He knew exactly where he was, and what he was doing, and he didn't appear to be paranoid about being there. He seemed to understand, as outcasts often do, that he was feared by others and therefore he had nothing himself to fear.

"Don't die tonight," a guard told me minutes before I walked out of prison to freedom. His words were a warning against the outside world, a world I had been separated from by the prison wall. "There's plenty of time to die. Do it later, not tonight." He was talking about the dangers of the city's streets—juveniles with shotguns; crack dealers fighting over territorial rights; cops with hair-trigger guns—accidents that can be avoided; but he could just as well have been warning me about AIDS.

"Everybody plays the lottery, but nobody plays with AIDS," Ruth, a well-known bioethicist, told me. "AIDS," she said, "has changed the ways people relate." Dress and lifestyle are still designed to attract. People speak in double entendres and drip sexual innuendos. But AIDS keeps people away from each other. "It's confusing," Ruth said, "and there are few places to find sanctuary from the confusion."

Before leaving prison, I was tested twice for AIDS. Although homosexuality and drug abuse are realities in prison, neither appealed to me. I hadn't engaged in any high-risk behaviors and had no doubts I'd test HIV negative. Still, to make a statement, I insisted on being tested. My initial request was turned down by the medical staff. They had no procedure for voluntary testing. The more red tape I encountered, the more determined I was to be tested. Other inmates also wanted to be tested, especially those with a history of IV drug use, but they took the first "No" as final and didn't pursue the issue. But I did, and finally I met a prison doctor who agreed with me: voluntary testing should be allowed in prison.

My tests came back clean, and now that I'm out of prison, I'm like a eunuch in a world where sex had once been a revolutionary obligation. Only a deathstruck fool visits a casual bed today. Promiscuity is a thing of the past, a dance done at arm's length.

Not long after I went to prison, I woke in the middle of the night and sat up on the side of my bed. The cell was so quiet I could hear cockroaches foraging in my garbage.

"When I get out of prison," I said to myself, "sex can wait." Thinking of what I would most like to do, I said, "I'm going to eat strawberries! Big! Fresh! Red strawberries!" And that became my mantra for the rest of the time I was in prison.

On the day I was released, Kathrin, a friend, a sister, my confidante, came to pick me up. She was there with her camera, taking photos of me as I walked through the last gate to freedom. She drove me to the house where she lived with her husband and son, and fed me steamed shrimp, French champagne and *strawberries!*

I have flashbacks to my sixteen years, three months in prison. I walk the street and catch a whiff of an odor, or I see something from the corner of my eye—an expression on a face in a crowded subway car—and the horrors of prison are with me again. A clear, hard reminder. The flashbacks are as unwelcome as those of the Vietnam combat veteran. Handcuffs, shackles, steel bars, cold cells, bland food, brutal guards, indifferent officials. Every encounter was accompanied by the possibility of sudden death.

At times, I'm not sure if the flashbacks to prison are more, or less, frightening than the desperation I see on the faces of people in the free world around me. Perhaps, in time, I'll become inured, insensitive, even jaded and will no longer see in detail the world around me. Then I'll be resocialized, readjusted and just like everybody else—a prisoner of my own desperation, a prisoner in a prison without walls.

Index of Named Pieces